The Invitation

Uncovering God's Longing to Be Heard

FRANNIE ROSE

BALBOA.
PRESS

A DIVISION OF HAY HOUSE

Author Credits
Sue Lion, artist; Suzanne D'Acquisto, photographer

Balboa Press books may be ordered through booksellers or by contacting:

Balboa Press
A Division of Hay House
1663 Liberty Drive
Bloomington, IN 47403
www.balboapress.com
1 (877) 407-4847

Print information available on the last page.

ISBN: 978-1-5043-2867-8 (sc)
ISBN: 978-1-5043-2869-2 (hc)
ISBN: 978-1-5043-2868-5 (e)

Library of Congress Control Number: 2015903251

Balboa Press rev. date: 4/1/2015

With all my heart, I give this book to God,
for this is His story.
My prayer is for Him to do with it as He wishes.
And I share it with the love of my life, Frank,
who stood beside me
while witnessing in wonder
this miraculous transformation as it occurred.

The Messenger

On a foggy, feather-coated day
of dream-like reality
hidden between moments of clarity and pain,
a woman remembers
the journey her feet have traveled
while she wonders
why all at once
the world stopped,
leaving her stranded in loneliness.

He comes prancing in as a Messenger
through the forest of pine trees
to give her the Light from within His eyes.
But she does not look up from her own pain
to see His strong body standing tall,
waiting
for her to notice.

Tears fall from her deep brown eyes
as she struggles through past and future,
regrets in focus
while she anticipates future plans,
mind pictures, and memories.
As the present moment passes slowly by her,
she sits within her fog
pondering feelings of lack and emptiness.

With the gentle breeze
a gate outside her yard
is quietly blown wide open
as the Messenger once again travels toward her

in the darkening dusk
as evening appears.
The only light seen is deep within His eyes.
Walking toward her, He gazes gracefully above Him
with the hope in His heart
that, finally, she will look His way.

She stares into space, focusing on nothing
but her thoughts
as He stands tall with great strength and massive antlers.
Not once does her head raise
to look out into His Presence.
In front of her eyes, He stands unseen.

The Messenger leaves with His message of Light
as an empty woman cries,
"Where are You, God?
Why have You abandoned me?"
Never once looking up into the Light--
the Light shining brightly
from the Messenger's eyes.

—Frannie Rose

CONTENTS

PART I: THE JOURNEY
INTRODUCTION TO THE JOURNEY — 3

PART II: THE TEACHINGS
THE TRUTH IN THE TEACHINGS:
AN INVITATION TO THE HEART OF THE READER — 93

Foreword

I first met Frannie Rose a little less than five years ago when she approached me at a hospital dinner and asked if I would be free to see her sometime. My first thought was that she would be seeking spiritual direction from me, as a few people do, and that we might strike up that kind of relationship.

God works in wondrous, different ways! It was, in fact, Frannie who made an invitation to me that she would help me to listen for God's voice in my life if it were something my heart would wish. It took me some time to respond to her, because frankly, I wasn't certain that I did wish to hear God's voice. Somewhere along the line, I had determined that God usually asks what is difficult, and I wasn't certain that I was up to that kind of challenge.

After two months of prayer, I was unable to rid my heart of the desire to hear more from her. Her story, as related in this book, touched my heart and convinced me that what she was experiencing was authentically of God.

In March of 2009, I began to work with Frannie. I have since learned to hear God's voice in my own life and have discovered a depth of joy I never thought possible. I can verify that the teachings Frannie shares in her book certainly apply to my own inner journey.

The reader is invited to look at life in a new way. Though we all treasure our minds, and frankly, fear any diminishment of our minds, nonetheless, as Frannie teaches, the mind can truly get in the way. She explores what she has heard from God in regard to the pursuit of the *Self* that God intends for us to be. In her experience and in mine as well, our minds and our hearts tend to work at cross-purposes because of the secular world in which we live. According to secular society, the mind produces and the heart confuses. On the contrary, the heart is open to receive the love of God, and the mind is prone to dissect the experience of love and leave it ineffective.

The reader will often be challenged to examine the values, and manners of pursuing those values, that dominate their lives at present. To the soul who longs for God's love, and the experience of that love, Frannie's book will be a confirmation of what God is asking of the longing heart.

Readers will find themselves facing what Frannie calls "the mind/heart conflict." In the early stages of the book, one might be tempted to think that Frannie is anti-mind. On the contrary, she says later in the work, "The purpose of your mind is to use it when *you* wish to use it, not let it use you."

The reader will be moved by the teachings Frannie has received from God that call for the longing soul to move to its heart, and there, to seek the experience of God and hear His voice. Her teachings, though centuries after Saint Bonaventure wrote *The Journey of the Mind to God*, sound very much like Bonaventure's learnings from God:

> We must suspend all the operations of the mind, and we must transform the peak of our affections, directing them to God alone. This is a sacred mystical experience. It cannot be comprehended by anyone unless he surrenders himself to it; nor can he surrender himself to it unless he longs for it; nor can he long for it unless the Holy Spirit, whom Christ sent into the world, should come and inflame his innermost soul....
>
> If you ask how such things can occur, seek the answer in God's grace, not in doctrine; in the longing of the will, not in the understanding; in the sighs of prayer, not in research; seek the bridegroom not the teacher; God and not man; darkness not daylight; and look not to the light but rather to the raging fire that carries the soul to God with intense fervor and glowing love...

When the heart can no longer speak in prosaic terms, it becomes a poet. Frannie is one of those. May all who read this work come to the center where Frannie invites us to live. Peace in the world will only be found from the center outward. The world needs to hear God's poets.

Bishop Richard Charles Patrick Hanifen
Bishop Emeritus
Colorado Springs, Colorado

Acknowledgments

The process of writing this book easily became a living braid of three strands: God; the people who have supported, helped, and loved me into continuing with this story; and the new depth of my heart. I wish to open this heart and share my love and gratitude with the following people:

I thank my dear Frank, who loved me before this experience and continues to love me after—watching with amazement as I experience God, and caring enough to ask me to share with him what I have learned. By doing so, he learned how to hear God's voice, as now he, too, listens to God every moment.

I thank Sean for the beautiful wisdom and deep love that manifests through his incredible, creative passion. His music was always the background to this story, and his love, always unconditional. Now that he, too, hears God's voice, I believe a rich and fruitful life will unfold for him.

I thank Ryan, who vowed to become a better man and doctor than many of those I encountered in the long years of my illness. Through this commitment, he has now begun to pursue soul-touching medicine. While listening to God, he has seen incredible possibility.

I thank my wondrous doctor and healer, Joel S. Levine, for his perseverance, expertise, and caring through all these years—for without him and God, this book would never have been possible. The enduring faith I see in his eyes was always known by my heart.

I thank Sister Nancy Hoffman for her love of God, for taking the chance to hear Him, and for always listening. Without her commitment to God and her sweet friendship, much of what has followed in this story would not have been possible.

I thank Bishop Richard Hanifen for his spiritual friendship, faith, and love for God, as once he began to listen, a new life grew from within his heart, nurtured by God's words to him. What he has taught me has deepened and enriched my life.

My gratitude goes out to Lisa Curtis for editing this manuscript with the faith that it will touch others as it touched her. I thank her for her faith in me and for her never-ending encouragement. As God's words unfold for her, revealing a new life, I wish her always to be as free as I have become.

I thank Becca for adding to my family a new and fresh ear and for her love, goodness, and encouragement throughout this endeavor.

I thank Britta for always with a smile saying the things that bring my heart to laughter, even in the most complicated moments.

I feel such gratitude for Sue Lion, who has always been a tremendous creative force in my life, with her vision and mine always aligned. Her artwork speaks prophetically to me of our eventual meeting. She captures my heart in every stroke of her brush.

And lastly, I thank my fellow journeyers who have been part of *One Simple Voice*: Jerry Bagg, Larry Barrett, Andy Barton, Mike Boyd, Dick Campbell, Father Bill Carmody, Charles Coon, Marc Crawford, Margaret Deiotte, Monsignor Donald Dunn, Jim Felix, Liz Follen, Gary Foote, Ed Gaffney, Marcia Gasper, Sally Hegarty, Lynn Hurst, Ron Kinder, Sister Lou Krippel, Father Ken Przybyla, Dianne Reitan, Sister Dorothy Schlaeger, Monsignor John Slattery, Father Paul Wicker, all our heartfelt volunteers, and the many thousands of retreatants who have attended our workshops and retreats, learning to hear God's voice. May you always walk with His words in your heart and follow His meaning and purpose for you.

To the Reader

I give to you a wondrous gift in the pages ahead—not something tangible to follow, like a list or a how-to book—but an experience you will never forget. And as you read through these pages, this story will soon become yours.

Never for one moment in the seventeenth year of my bedridden life would I have imagined the life that awaited me. Never would I have thought that I was about to walk into wonder—a life filled with color and wild imaginings. My limited mind told me that I would get what I always got and that each day would be lived as the day before—imprisoned forever with a wish in my heart to be free.

Let this story be for you a testament that faith is the secret to living an extraordinary, unexpected, wondrous life—and that in the worst, most unimaginable struggles, a gift awaits you. For no matter how hard your life is and how desperate you become, together with God, all good things are possible. It's simple: if you look for the open door, a mystical life is waiting for you.

In God's peace and love,
Frannie Rose
July 23, 2014

"It is in the silence of the heart that God speaks."
—Mother Teresa

"Today if ye will hear His voice, harden not your heart."
—Psalm 95:7b–8a (King James Version)

"It is written,
'Man shall not live by bread alone,
but by every word that proceedeth out of the mouth of God.'"
—Matthew 4:4 (King James Version)

"That which God said to the rose,
and caused it to laugh in full-blown beauty,
He said to my heart, and made it a hundred times more beautiful."
—Rumi

PART

I

The Journey

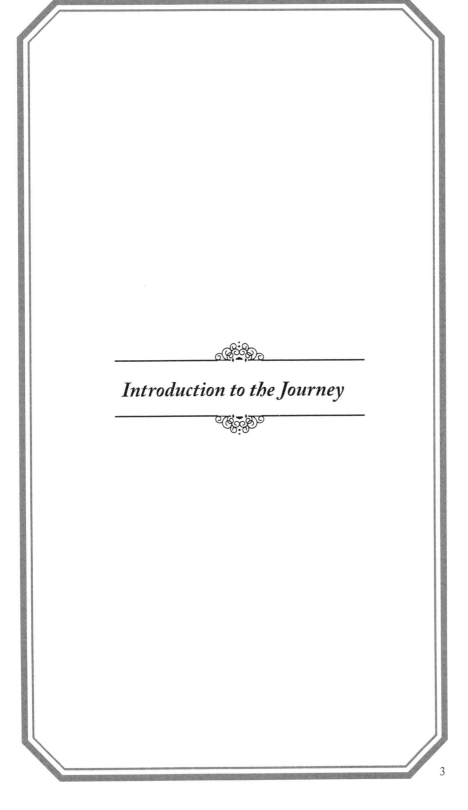

Introduction to the Journey

In 1990, while I lay in my bed, I could do little more than draw chalk designs on a sketchpad. I remember creating two drawings—one of a woman's neck with a sparkling necklace and another of several straight-lined buildings in a city. These were very simple drawings in the brightest of colors. There was no detail, only lines moving in different directions. These lines were simple, and they took little concentration. Though I was cognitively impaired at the time, I still remember the thoughts I had while drawing these pictures and the images I wished to create.

Six months before completing this book, I had an afternoon with nothing to do. I decided not to plan anything that day, for I wished to see what might grow out of the emptiness. I went into the garage, and not liking its cold dampness, I opened the large door facing the mountains. Sunlight fell upon a shelf so that a white box, labeled "1990," caught my eye. Feeling pulled to this box, I opened it. Touching the weakened rubber band until it snapped, and opening a roll of artwork, I was coaxed by the bright colors and enchanted by its fairytale quality. There in my hands was the only thing left from my bed during seventeen years of illness.

As I uncovered these drawings, I remembered clearly my intention when I drew them. Yet, at the time I created these designs, they had been unrecognizable to me. Only this day, in the cold, damp garage, did I see the resemblance of these drawings to a diagram God recently had given me in a vision. I was told it was the origin of the human spirit. It didn't take long to realize that this diagram was the very same drawing I had sketched from my bed in 1990. Now in wellness, it came to me with labels from God. This moment in the garage was beyond words. How could

I have been so sick, and yet, casually have created these exact drawings?

In the old roll of pages, there were other drawings—of buildings I now recognized as churches. I remember my intention at that time had been to draw buildings. I was raised a Jew, and churches were not what I drew in those days. Churches were nonexistent in my life or in my consciousness. Yet this day in the garage, I could see that while so very ill, I unconsciously had drawn churches with crosses on the doors and large steeples on the rooftops.

Before seeing these drawings and since becoming well, I have been working in churches—the very same churches that were in those drawings from 1990. I could come up with no explanation for this. It confounded me. The drawings I found in the garage from a time I was living in bed were prophetic. The deepest of all messages were in this reality. God's wish for me—my destiny—was in this reality.

What I realized on that empty day in the garage is this: that we never fully awaken to the sacredness of our lives. God sits with us each and every day from within the emptiness. The seventeen years of sickness was not downtime. God had been working inside me. While I thought I was wasting my life in the void and emptiness of illness, God had been busy. I was being kept confined in a cocoon, while inside, a butterfly was being woven from my heart. One day, when the sky was bright and the wind was perfect, my heart burned through the cocoon, and God set a butterfly free.

CHAPTER 1

New Birth Begins as Chaos

I sit here now in total silence, a child in a middle-aged body, staring up at blue skies and mountaintops. Clouds enter this view from time to time, passing slowly by my window and then leaving the bluest of skies behind. I see the mountaintops sugarcoated with snow, for this is the season of winter and rest. Yet beneath this frozen layer, a new beginning emerges, deeper than my distant sight allows me to see. The ground is preparing for a lush and fragrant springtime. The soil that has been nurtured, watered, and shined upon is sprouting new growth, its roots established firmly deep under the ground, out of sight.

While feeling this in my heart, I recognize that we, too, are like this. Our roots grow and sprout underneath a layer of cold snow, yet we know that new growth is occurring away from view. It is happening all the time, as we are showered and nurtured with life experiences, the lessons from which we learn. The snow covering is the only thing that keeps us from the sparkling light of the sun. And although the sun is trying hard to burn through it to find us, we sometimes believe the world of snow covering is the only world that is.

The warmth of the sun penetrates through the snow covering for each of us, and when, finally, we feel it on our faces, a new world unfolds. It is a world of beauty, a world of miracles, and a world of love that is unseen to our eyes, but known by our hearts. Some see this world at their time of death. Others have awareness that it exists throughout their lives. Some never experience it, hiding deep beneath the shady bushes for fear of being torn from the comfort of their conditioned lives.

In 1986, I was a successful professional woman with two small toddlers. I had a master's degree and a wondrously exciting career. One day, I suddenly became ill. It really was quite simple: I could not get out of my bed. At first, I rested so that I could recover. But when days turned into weeks, I went to the doctor for some kind of relief. Later, I received word that all my tests had come back fine. I continued to sleep, waiting for wellness to find me. Weeks turned into months as the structure of medicine collapsed on me. I went from doctor to doctor to find what was wrong, but there were no answers.

Months turned into chaotic years as I lay bedridden with two small toddlers. It was sad and frustrating that what kept me in bed had no name, no treatment, and no reality to the doctors and those around me. My friends and family tired of the ordeal and spoke candidly. They were visibly impatient, pushing me to get out of my bed, as if my lying there were too hard for them to endure. They asked me to stop seeing doctors—for me, the equivalent of abandoning my only hope. Family and friends fell in and out of my life. Some lost interest in me, and others did not know what to say or do. Years turned into a decade, and I began to wonder if loved ones had been right to leave me. I was afraid I was dying, and I feared what would happen to my children, to my husband, and to me.

By this time, what had been my life had lost all meaning. Before this illness, I worked hard to achieve and obtain all the things I had, never really appreciating success. I had been conditioned to work obsessively toward a future. Bedridden, I had been forced to give up my career and everything for which I had worked in my life. Somehow I raised two babies from my bed, later tutoring them in their homework as many years passed before us. I was not able to take walks, to play in the yard, or to tend to their active lives. Missing out on a normal life, my husband lived with anxiety about what was wrong with me. Life for each of us had stopped dead in its tracks.

After seventeen years of loss and chaos, lying in bed and going from doctor to doctor, I felt that time was running out. In a frozen-in-time moment, sunlight streamed through the curtains, and I looked out a north-facing bedroom window, viewing life going on without me. The dichotomy was pronounced. As I felt my hope fade, I watched the sun dance on my curtains, trying to tantalize me outside, yet I had to lie there in a bed prison, feeling helpless, lost, and forgotten. I had a choice, simple but true: I could lie in my bed forever, as I was, an option more frightening than any other; I could kill myself and end my life of misery; or I could surrender to a God I felt had abandoned me all those years.

It was a hard and painful choice to make. A simple solution would have been to end it all and free my husband and my children to go on with their lives in a more active way. I knew that lying there was no longer a choice I wished to make; a life in a bed was not quality of life. So through the process of elimination, I chose between surrender and death. And through much suffering and foggy thought, I simply chose to surrender to God.

At that moment of surrender, my bed became sacred ground. I lay there with my heart wide open and empty, for I had lost all that I thought I was. I lay there and waited for a God of whom I was not sure to help me live. In that unusually lucid moment, a breeze came flowing through my window, fragrantly familiar. I not only smelled it; I felt it—a unique aroma, and one I had sensed in my life as a small child. The fragrance smelled like hope to me.

Within a matter of days, I received a call from the nurse of a doctor I had been trying to see for years. She told me that this doctor wished to set up an appointment to see me at a special clinic. With hope in my heart that I had not felt for a decade, I set up the appointment and patiently waited for that day to come. I spent all that time waiting, with blind faith, in total surrender to a God I never knew—a God I hoped was listening to me.

From the time I saw that doctor to this present moment, a metamorphosis has occurred that only those around me who were witness to it could affirm. Dr. Jones led me to Dr. Slocumb—synchronously a doctor about whom I had read years earlier and who had, that very week, moved to town from a faraway place. Dr. Slocumb treated me and sent me to Dr. Levine, who diagnosed me and began treatment for a rare and hard-to-diagnose disease called systemic mastocytosis. Within a year of my meeting Dr. Levine, I was out of my bed, walking a mile through my neighborhood every day with new eyes. I was walking across the bridge by the lake that overlooked the tallest of snowy mountaintops with the eyes of a child.

And so it is with these new eyes, after lying in bed for almost seventeen years, that I write this book. It is with these new eyes, after my surrender to a God whose existence I questioned, that I broke free of the brittle covering that surrounded me and the frozen ground of adversity. As each sprout of heart emerged, I felt on my back the warmth of the sun, and as life gained strength within the covering, I felt the sun coaxing me to move away from the underground life that illness had created for me. As I moved upward through the soil, the sun was melting the snow on the mountaintops, exposing thick, lush new growth to the spring air. I saw it all from the empty garden in which I now found myself. I saw every sprout and every blossom around me grow. Nothing in this world could ever shake that knowing, because I was there. It happened to me. From the chaos of a forgotten life, I experienced a miracle.

Within these pages, I share with you the wisdom that came to me, the journey that greeted me from the emptiness of this sacred ground, and the wondrous story of majesty that continues to unfold.

CHAPTER 2

The End Is Where We Start From

No one could have prepared me for the emptiness I would feel when I walked back into my life. It was something I did not expect. I knew there was so much for which to be grateful. The wish I had for seventeen years had been granted to me by God, and now, I had richer soil in which to grow healthy. I looked at the soil and saw no visible growth, and I knew I had nothing to plant into it. All I had before was now pulled from the garden, and I was left with emptiness.

There I stood. Time had come to an awkward halt as I looked into the mirror, finally seeing the truth. All this time, I had been in denial and resistance to moving forward in my life. It seemed the best things I had were now over: I was no longer a speech pathologist; my children were grown and in college; and my husband had made do by himself. I wondered why it had to end. Why did something so wonderful as my life before illness come to an end?

Our human world is a world of transience. Things come, and things go through our lives. There is nothing of life that promises us permanence, and yet, our minds believe the illusion that everything is supposed to remain the same. Nothing remains the same. Everything changes, flowing from one place to another—into our hands and then away from our hands.

My mind told me that when something flowed away from me, I was empty. To the mind's eye, emptiness is a state of lack. I lacked having "something" within that space to fill it. What made emptiness even harder to accept was that I had defined my false self by having filled space, filled time, and a filled home. This is how we get a sense of self or a sense of ego—and how we become distracted in our lives. I had searched for things "outside" myself—things that only can be found to be permanent and eternal when found "inside."

The wondrous hope in my heart saw this emptiness as a place to begin—a clean sheet of paper on which to create a life that I had only imagined and longed for, a field of infinite possibility. But when I listened to my mind, that empty sheet of paper and that empty space had "no thing" of value.

T. S. Eliot, the great poet, wrote in his masterpiece, *The Four Quartets*, "What we call the beginning is often the end. And to make an end is to make a beginning. The end is where we start from." He spoke of the knowing that a new beginning is often an ending. He spoke of an ending as the wondrous emptiness from which we start. But in order to start, instead of resisting what already is, we must step forward on faith—a faith that we are not alone in starting. We must remember that we are one with the Creator of all things, especially in our creation of a new life, as He is creating with us. He is using our life as a pencil on that blank sheet of paper—His canvas. And we have a precious opportunity to hold His pencil with Him so His beautiful artistry may flow through us the way that He wishes it to be.

At home, at work, or even in love, endings are simply beginnings in disguise. We see the hint of excitement within our hearts when we feel a new beginning. There is a sense of opportunity and a knowing that anything wonderful and good can happen. The mind can take us to fear, but the heart only wishes to run with opportunity—to run wild like a child runs through an open field, feeling the power of his own legs moving him forward. As the power of God pulses within his heart and pumps strength and life-feeding blood through his veins, the field becomes one of infinite potential!

Standing amidst my new reality, I flipped my fears and resistance around to see the emptiness in my life as a fresh new canvas. I painted my life freely, with God's help, in the infinite colors of a rainbow. I painted with deep faith, hope, and love. I sensed I would find this ending on which I'd been focused as a wondrous new beginning in disguise—a masterpiece painted by "We"—God and me. When I finally realized this, it was time to give this emptiness—this new beginning—every fiber of my heart.

CHAPTER 3

The Emptiness Is Space to Grow

All new growth is a movement from confined space and eventual discomfort to a place of emptiness, freedom, and space to be. It is always a movement from the darkness in the direction of light. A garden begins with emptiness on the outside, but underneath the ground, there is much going on. The tiny seeds planted begin to sprout and move upward toward the light of the sun, eventually breaking ground and moving into an area of more space so this seed might open up wide into joyous blossom.

All creation begins with emptiness. When we begin a project, we begin with nothing but the supplies we need. The eye does not yet know what beauty will be created. Then, from the nothingness comes something. Our spirits begin to create, and the project grows both in beauty and in substance. From nothing does indeed come something.

For seventeen years while I lay in my bed with illness, I felt emptiness. Slowly, I was being rid of the shell I had once chosen to surround me—the shell of what I was. I no longer could work at the profession for which I had been prepared and educated. My role and function as a wife and mother had been replaced with an identity of one who was ill. And by the time the cause of my illness finally was determined, all possible "identities" were gone. I was left with few memories from seventeen years during which the world went on without me. I could either catch up with it or begin anew. I did not wish to spend another second in this life waiting to live. For me, this emptiness was my new beginning.

None of us remembers what it felt like to be born—to be set free from the small circle of life that bound us, to exit the womb, and to encounter the world for the very first time. We did not know to expect anything. We only knew that we were bursting out of something we somehow had outgrown. There was not enough space in which to grow or to live, and we were not able to breathe. Stifled in the womb, we edged slowly toward a place of space, without awareness of the gifts that awaited us.

There was discomfort in moving through the period of feeling confined and thwarted, and great distress in moving through the narrow pathway of the birth canal. In other words, things got worse for us before they got better. Yet we continued to venture through this birth canal, pushing through the discomfort and pain, finding our way to the other side. We found our way to freedom—out of that world and into this world—into the light.

There were many options that God could have given other than this journey out. We might have resisted this journey, unmoving from the safety and security of that soft place in which we lay, and even though we were too big for that space, we might have remained in that spot. Yet we did not know enough to be given a choice. It was God's choice to bring us to life. Somehow, through the grace of God, we moved forward through the pain to be born and into the light.

Our inner journey is like this. Sometimes, metaphorically, our space becomes too confined. We may feel enough of a sense of restriction about our lives that we feel pulled to journey inward where there is more space to grow deeper and be. Sometimes we feel as though we are in a place of great discomfort. We can only see the past and the present, and we cannot see where we are headed. But the difference here is that we each have a mind that thinks, and the mind has a will of its own. Though the natural course of the journey is to push through the pain, our minds will not let us. Instead, they turn back and tell us that the journey forward is too hard for us to bear. And so we sit in this same place for a very long time, finding a way to stay in the small spot where we lie. Though it constricts us, we feel at ease with the restrictions. Because we know them, we find comfort in them and think it's better than taking the unknown risk of moving in any direction, especially toward a place our minds foresee as emptiness. Within the familiar restrictions, we think we know what will be, and we think we can create the same outcome every day, because we fear change. We fear the unknown in our lives. We see the unknown as emptiness, and more than anything else in our lives, we fear emptiness.

Once recovering from the seventeen years in bed, I began to walk down the streets of my neighborhood. I had a strong and intense awareness of all the space around me. Looking up at the palest blue sky, sometimes without clouds to veil my view, I felt the essence of great space outside of me connecting with new space within me. I was emptiness looking out into the emptiness for the very first time in my life. I was acutely aware of exactly how this felt—the sweet and gentle peace that blanketed me as I made this internal to external connection. I had an inner knowing that it was all the same substance—inside and outside of me, all the same energy—and most importantly, this emptiness was meant to be there.

CHAPTER 4

The Truth of Who I Am

The journey of living life in this world metaphorically parallels the life of an embryo. We awaken in a world that we come to know. It becomes a world of probability, and simply by thinking we will, we can create specific outcomes. We automatically take actions to make these outcomes reality. In fact, we do the same things day in and day out, because we think there is comfort in routines. We fool ourselves into thinking that these routines produce outcomes we have created, and this becomes positive reinforcement for continuing to use them. Routines become habits. Our minds tell us habits are hard to break. Therefore, we remain within the same space, doing the same things at the same times.

However, unbeknownst to us, there is a part of us that wishes to grow and move from this space of comfort. It is the part of us that pushed us out of the birth canal. It is the power of life itself. This spark of life connects with our Creator and connects with all living things conceived by this Creator. God gave each of us the life force within, a piece of God-Self. As we journey through our lives, this life calls us through our hearts, wishing to break free to other worlds, as we did on our journey from embryo to birth as a human being.

So what really happens to our spark of life from the time of birth? Spiritually speaking, it is born with new and empty eyes, the eyes of a child. From the moment we come into this world, all that is truth to us is what we can sense of the present moment. There is not yet recognition of cause and effect. There is only now, this moment and none other. We exist, we are, and we are in a state of being. This state portrays the words "I Am." Life is. It is as simple as that. And by saying, "Life is," God is saying, "God is."

Within the center of our spirits lies this connection to God, this "I Am" that exists in the total awareness of the present moment and exists as life itself, a piece or connection to God. We each live as this existence and this awareness as our "heart center" develops around it. The heart center contains the seeds to a wondrous garden planted within us by our Creator. In other words, God is in the middle of the heart center, and together, we call this spiritual center "the true Self."

Remembering that the embryo was once what might be compared with a seed, so, too, is the heart center. In truth, we each are created to blossom and grow, no differently than a beautiful flower. We do not exist to stop growing. We burst into existence *to be*, to grow, and to create more life—to manifest as life itself. These beautiful seeds are the seeds of love, goodness, joy, hope, compassion, faith, peace, generosity, gratitude, freedom, and so many beautiful components of the world of the unmanifested. They lie within us, slowly growing to flower and bear fruit so we may give to the world freely. This is who we are. This is our true Self. This is the gift of life that we have been given—a gift from within which to blossom, to grow, and to create.

As I walked with the emptiness within me and outside of me, I felt great peace. My awareness of nature became amplified, widened, and deepened. I listened to the sounds of a bird's wings as it flew through the air, imagined what it would feel like to be a small insect in a bright orange flower, watched the ants visit their friends in the sidewalk, and felt the trees as they bent with the breezes. For a time, I felt my emptiness deepening, but rising to the surface was a heart unburdened and filled with great hope. There was nothing in my mind of how this time was supposed to be. There was only the present moment, this *now* in which I was alive. I lived it one second at a time; it gave me great peace and silence from the years of echoing thoughts and judgments about what had been my life.

While walking each day, my heart was dauntless and daring, rising to the top of my being. There was nothing about which to think—only the wondrous sky and the silence that surrounded me. It was perhaps in one of those moments that I felt my mind becoming restless, and I knew there were questions to be answered—questions of purpose and meaning. While I walked on in this beauty-filled mountain town, life was going on around me. People were busy doing, and I had nothing to do. I no longer possessed the identity of a sick person, yet I did not identify as a well person either. With some time to journey on, I asked myself simply, "Who am I?"

At that time, there clearly were two of me—my true Self and my ego (the one I knew as me). I was well aware of the difference.

One was content to be, to live, and to journey on in peace, love, and goodness, while the other was striving to maintain an identity I no longer even possessed. In an instant, I realized I had lost my identity through the years of illness, and I realized I did not wish to carry the empty shell of any identity I had carried before. Again, I came to a place of making choices. Who was I? A voice rang back in my head with reassurance, and it said clearly and peacefully, "Whomever you wish to be, dear girl."

In that moment, I realized that I was about to make a most important choice. I could be "what I was," or I could be "who I was." Since what I was clearly had been cracked and crumbled, and only joy and peace remained, I would live my life as who I was: the heart center—"We"—God and I together, filled with love, peace, compassion, goodness, and all the wondrous beauty-filled seeds planted deep within my heart. Yes, that was who I was. That is my true Self, who I was meant to be.

CHAPTER 5

A Heart Awakens

When I look at a toddler or a young child, I see wonder in his eyes. The sparkle that comes from the light as it shines on that wonder is what catches one's attention. Little children breathe to us that light which is life and bring us face to face with the deepest part of ourselves. This part, the true Self, is what we have covered up with what we perceive as the reason for being: have tos, searching, and things to do. A child's wonder comes from being empty and unfilled inside, while remaining naturally open to all that he feels.

Somewhere along the way, children learn to fill up the emptiness that is so essential to feeling their own hearts. As a squirrel often buries a nut in the dirt with the intention of returning to it later, we do the same. But what happens with the nuts that are buried? Often, the squirrel forgets where he puts them, and he spends many a day in the cold winter searching for nuts he stashed away somewhere outside. What is the difference between the squirrel and a human being? We have lost our innocence in a deeper but more accessible place—inside of us. And we spend our whole lives in the futile search for it *outside* of ourselves.

What is innocence? It is seeing the world through openness and emptiness. When we view the world from our hearts, we are able to see more than we ever could imagine. There is space for the heart to rise to the top of our being and to expand in its natural way, the way it was meant to expand.

The playfulness of a child begins with emptiness that is at the root of innocence. There is space for creativity, for games, and for the act of fun. In children, the mind is not experienced enough to interfere. It is simply out of openness that "being" occurs. And "being" is the state of openness where heart seeds blossom and freedom thrives.

While I was sick and lying in bed, I had much to fill me. I had the mystery of an illness that doctors could not diagnose, and I had physical pain about which to think. Yet at a certain point in the search for the answer, my mind quit the futile task, and emptiness was the result. There was nothing else I could do but surrender to that emptiness. When I did so, my heart rose up to expand and open.

Now that my life has been forcibly slowed, I can see how the world functions. Living through my heart, I can feel once again the innocence of a child, and when I lose that center, I quickly empty and connect with the space around me. I feel always with emptiness and openness the peace of my heart as it opens to take in the world.

The trees stand beautifully tall, reaching the blue skies. The squirrels work to find food in the early mornings, and they rest from noon to midafternoon on tree branches. Their eyes are not closed to the world, but perched on these branches, the squirrels observe the goings on around them. They pause to take in and open to the world without having to be a certain way or do anything. The Colorado crows fly toward the east before sunrise, and they sit on the tallest treetops together, chattering away, but as the sun comes up in its awesome splendor, the crows stop in silence and watch for minutes before flying away to their daytime destinations. In the evenings before sunset, they find the tallest trees in the west and chatter away together. When the sun finally goes down behind the mountaintops, they are silent once again to be with that present moment.

As I wandered outside my home for the first time in seventeen years, with no past to guide me and too young in freedom for future wants and desires, I knew that living from my heart—my true Self— was the most meaningful lesson so far on the journey to wellness. Knowing that this was my lesson to learn, and my lesson to never forget, I honored that lesson every day by creating time for my heart to blossom and grow. There was nothing more important or anything that deserved my attention more. I was alive!

CHAPTER 6

One Simple Voice

As this journey of wonder continued, I took the same walk every day through my quiet neighborhood overlooking the Rocky Mountains. I walked on residential streets to a bridge that crossed a small lake facing an old community church. Each day, as I walked over the bridge, the view of the purple mountains and the lake before them was most beautiful. It took me to an old, lush church garden overlooking this wondrous view where I often sat in quiet meditation of the surrounding majesty. In the springtime, I could sit there for hours as I listened to the calls of the Canadian geese. In wonder, I watched them descend, time after time, their feet gently touching the glassy water as they skidded in for a landing. The morning sounds of the doves and the red-winged blackbirds through the surrounding pine trees and scrub oaks rocked me awake to the magic of life.

I hadn't prayed a day in my life, as my heart never rose to organized religion. It sparked instead to the twinkle in people's eyes when they spoke of those they love, God included. Until that day of surrender, God and I had been separate. I felt no connection. It was as though I was estranged from some part of me that I had refused to know, and that was the part of me with which I began to connect in these sacred church gardens, down by the lake, listening to the sounds of the geese.

I sat there many days, deeply attending to the sounds of nature, and with time, I listened deeper inside my heart. Feeling an eternal innocence and seeing with the eyes of a child, I had so many questions and so many dreams. There were dreams about helping the world. There was wonder about my growing feelings of gratitude emerging from this new chance at living. I had questions about what had happened to me and why. From this new heart that I had only begun to explore, I wondered how I might best serve a world that seemed oblivious to its heart. I asked these questions shyly inside a silent head, and as I asked them, I felt a passion in my heart of wishing to know the answers.

We all come to the place of looking backward and asking, "Why me?" Often, we ask with the identity of a victim—complaining, fearing, and never wishing for an honest answer. My asking was followed by deep silence and peace; I sat with the questions for a long time. The silence deepened over time, and one day, when I asked the questions with the passion to know the answers, from deep in the silence an answer came.

Through many tears, I asked, "Why did this happen to me?" The tears came slowly at first and then led to rhythmic, steady sobs. Overlooking the lake in deep silence, I sat patiently, and the words came at once, in one simple voice: " I will always be here and will answer you. I ask only that you pause long enough to listen."

The voice could not be identified in terms of quality, tone, or volume, yet it was clear to me. It was familiar, and I had a deeper knowing that it had spoken to me before. Relaxing in its calm, we sat together. I asked questions, and it answered profoundly and freely. Laughing to myself, I felt as though I had made a new friend, or as they say of children, an invisible playmate. Yet when the voice spoke, my heartbeat slowed, and I was blanketed in soft peace with new depths of open space all around me. It stirred my heart to smell the fragrance of hope, the very same fragrance I had sensed from my bed long before. Goose bumps covered my skin as the voice spoke in comforting ways, saying the things that my heart most wished to hear; never an unkind word or judgment was uttered. As I sat overlooking the lake in the lush church gardens that day, I listened. I listened, I felt peace, and I wondered—all with a depth of knowing that I was infinitely changed.

Though life events and situations were up and down, these walks to the lake became most important to me. Over time, when I was silent enough, the voice would speak all along the way, no longer isolated to the meditation garden outside the church. Many days, I looked forward to the walk over the bridge while looking up at the bluest of skies, watching red-tailed hawks fly and hearing this wondrous voice in my head.

On one serious day of thinking, my mind's judgment appeared in place of wonder. My mind touched upon fear, thinking this voice might be a sign of fallout from my years in bed. I anticipated that what I heard could be a sign of mental illness and that perhaps what seemed joyous to me would take me away from reality. I tried to steer away from this type of thinking, for nothing in my life before had given me such comfort.

It was many months after I first heard the voice that the inevitable question came to me. I knew I wanted to ask it, but I was conscious that whatever was speaking to me had never told me about itself. I was awake to the feeling that my heart had a deeper knowing of who the voice was. There were times I wished to ignore it, wanting some kind of recognizable framework . Having access to a mystery within me, my mind wanted to solve it, and the more my mind wanted, the less I heard from the voice. It was as if I had entered a land of paradox. The more I thought about the voice, the more I could no longer access it, and yet, I needed to access it to know who it was.

For a few weeks, I felt sidetracked with these notions. The walks became more like work, and the task became to hear the voice. The harder I tried, the more my head filled with noise—judgment, fears of loss, and feelings of unworthiness.

One foggy day, I walked through an earthbound cloud, one step at a time, over the bridge to the center. As I stood in awe of the veil that surrounded me, I heard the voice again, speaking loudly and clearly through the fog. My mind really could not discern where I was going because the fog was thick in both directions. There was no point in trying to see where I came from; all I could see was the thickness of the fog. Stepping forward, I could not see ahead of me. All I could see was the step I was taking in that now moment. As I stood on the bridge, the voice said, "All that is important, dear Frannie, is the step you are taking now."

In that moment, I let go of what the voice was, for my heart knew the truth of the message. Each step forward through the thickness of the fog was a step in the right direction; every step was integral to the journey I was taking. No step was more important than *this* step. I knew that the path was made by each step. There was no path to journey to or journey on; it was only the journey itself that mattered, and the voice spoke to me of what a wondrous journey it was.

In my lighter, more present moments, I decided to live with the mystery of what the voice was a little longer. I named the voice "Ed." Ed and I traveled together one step at a time, each day to deeper places of awareness. Each step had its own lessons and its own gifts, and when I asked the questions, Ed answered with profundity and wisdom that I knew I never had been taught before.

Several months after first hearing Ed's voice, I awoke unable to walk. Something painful and distracting had diverted my journey. A new medical situation took me away from the lush church garden and the bridge by the lake. I pulled off my path, because I needed to have back surgery in order to walk again. Hindsight would teach me that there were lessons in this I needed to learn. Several months of great pain kept me from my walks in majesty, and I longed for them through the surgery and my slow recovery. My longing grew stronger as I wished to spend time with Ed and hear why my journey had been derailed again.

It was many months before I could walk any distance again, and during that time, I learned to journal my feelings about this newest diversion on my path. I read inspirational books and saw within these ancient writings some of the same themes of which Ed had spoken. My heart fluttered with a deeper knowing that I somehow had access to something greater than I was. I used this knowing to aid my recovery, and I built up my walking to go the whole distance I had traveled in the past.

On the first day back to my walk through the greenery, I spoke to my old friend again. "Ed, are you there?" I asked hesitantly but received a hearty reply.

"Welcome back to your Self, dear Frannie. I have been waiting to hear from you again."

The peace that always fell, like goose down from the sky, was again upon me. I spoke to Ed about obstacles, and I spoke to him of change. He explained how change occurs all the time, without our ever fully, consciously realizing it. Change is a moment-to-moment occurrence, but human beings miss it while we are busy filling our space with thoughts and activities. We fool ourselves into believing that change only happens intermittently, and when we do notice it, we perceive it as a threat. Ed told me that change is part of each day and each minute and each moment we live. He told me that only our minds tell us change is bad, whereas in truth, change keeps us flexible and able to bend with the storms that blow through our lives.

I applied that to the storm I had just experienced of being unable to do what I had done before as I recovered from the surgery. Ed and I spoke of obstacles and how they really are nothing more than rocks on a path. He told me that our minds see them as a problem, but they are only part of the terrain on which we travel—and there are always ways to travel around difficult terrain. We spoke of how it is all in the way we perceive it; the true message of life is clouded by false perceptions. Ed told me to look for the gifts on the path, for they outshine any rock or boulder that stands in my way. Our talk continued on to how humans see the boulders on their paths as brick walls that keep them from walking forward and how many people pull off the path, waiting for the boulders to be removed. Ed mentioned that he knew I would no longer do that, because I had learned through my journey that the only way to move is to step in the direction of surrender, trusting that the answers will come to me.

There was something so eternal and so powerful about the things Ed told me that day, and as I walked each day to the same places, we spoke of similar and deeper yearnings I had known since early childhood. I felt fault-finding, judgment, and unworthiness burn away by this new insight he was giving me. I no longer felt limited within my mind of thoughts. Instead, a new kind of freedom emerged in my life. Days moved on, and as our talks continued, Ed and I spoke of many more things that, to my amazement, I soon found in books and ancient texts of every religion.

As these conversations were emerging and my true Self was finding its way to the surface of my being, I noticed the attraction of wildlife to my home. On a summer morning, I awakened to the sound of the most beautiful bird songs before sunrise. I ventured out of the door facing east and saw the Colorado crows lined up on trees for the sunrise. The excitement in their voices became the excitement

I brought to each day. Over time, deer came through my yard and stayed for days on end. They came when they were injured or sick, and I fed them apples until they were strong enough to go off on their own. These deer became my friends, and I sat with them in the mornings. We ate breakfast together, and I spoke to them kindly while they looked into my eyes. When summer came, and it was time for the deer to bear their young, many were born in my yard, and I watched them grow. All these animals became to my heart the gifts of my journey with Ed—this journey back to wellness and this journey of my true Self.

It was almost a full year after first hearing the voice that, with the certain knowing of the answer, I asked Ed who he was. I asked because I was ready to ask, as a red apple is ready to fall from a tree. He answered me vaguely, but in a way familiar to my inner knowing. Clearly gentle with his answer, he said, "I am. I always have been. I am who you wish me to be. I always will be."

Standing on the bridge, I felt a surge of love flow through my veins. Feeling the calm as my heart slowed, I knew God was with me, inside me, and able to help move me wherever I wished to go. With that knowing, I asked God a simple question—one with great passion and faith. His answer was something my heart had been waiting for my whole life.

"God, I have so much gratitude. I don't know what to do with all the gratitude I have. It is just bursting from my heart. I wish to give You something—something in return with this new energy and passion You have given me for this life. You helped me get out of my bed! You sent me to my doctors who took care of me! You gave me these beautiful gifts! You stood beside me the whole way and waited patiently for me to come to You! What can I do to help You?" My heart was beating wildly as I waited for an answer.

He spoke sincerely and with great concern. "What do you wish for, Frannie?"

Quickly and impulsively, I answered, "I do so wish for peace in this world."

"My sweet Frannie Rose, you always get what you wish for," he said kindly and lovingly. Then, there was a long pause as the wind blew wildly. "Teach them to hear Me."

My throat gulped the air that was all around me. I swallowed hard. My mind tried to go astray, for I had no idea who "they" were—these people I was to teach. I had no idea where they would come from or if they would come. I stood on that beautiful bridge overlooking the snow-capped mountains and the deep blue water while the little snapping turtles were swimming with their little feet on the surface of the lake. The lake grew wild as the winds began to blow. There were ripples of white-capped water everywhere. The poor turtles had to dive deep to avert them.

The eternal message He gave me that day became a leap of faith that I had to take. My heart knew He was the God within me. There was meaning and purpose in His message. Ed returned to me as God that day, and I knew my journey was a miracle. The gifts I had been given far outweighed the loss of seventeen years of my life. For now, I traveled on a path with the God to whom I had surrendered many years before, and He was taking me to a place of beauty, sacredness, and love. There were no other messages in my head at that time; they all had been erased. I felt the comfort of a blanket of softness envelop me and the peace of a God I never had known before. It was wondrous, and I felt safe and loved and whole.

CHAPTER 7

Leaps of Faith

Many weeks passed while I sat with the voice and spoke about my life and the journey I had been traveling. The voice spoke to me of beginning a practice of awakening and journaling my thoughts and fears to empty my mind of the past and future. God asked me to become aware of and to journal about the gifts of the present moment. I learned to ask God questions about my destiny. I began this practice by awakening at sunrise, listening to the birdcalls and the crows, and watching as a beauty-filled picture manifested in the sky with colored clouds and orange mountaintops. I followed the crows with the morning meditation at sunrise, and I felt awareness of the "givens" I had taken for granted almost all my life: the sunrise, the sky, the clouds, and the sun. Every morning, I greeted them with excitement and joy, never doubting their dependability or fearing their absence. They were symbols of the life I had found, and I could always look up at them to be reminded if I lost my center.

Challenging life situations occurred during this time, but I was able to see them as only inconveniences on my path, as the voice had told me that every path has rocky terrain from time to time. I carried such great peace that I was not often thrown by these situations; when I did get caught up in the world in which others lived, I found it hard to hear the voice at all. When this happened, I wondered if hearing the voice was merely my imagination, and when I went to this place of thinking, I lost all contact with the joy I had come to know. I missed these conversations, and I questioned: If, indeed, I had been speaking with God, why would He abandon me? I ventured deeper into thought, and finally, I stopped hearing the voice entirely. I had to know why.

I sat underneath the blue spruce tree that day, in the middle of the meditation garden at the church, and I cried. I cried for those seventeen years I had missed. Feeling the loss of my children as they grew up during that time, the tears continued to flow. But my most painful loss was not hearing God speak to me anymore. I wondered if I had done something wrong or if the voice had been only a figment of my imagination. I cried long and hard that day. Finally, I asked,

"God, where are You?" I sat quietly and listened for an answer, and an answer finally came.

"Frannie, I have been here all along. I am always with you. When you cannot hear Me, you are no longer in your heart. The human mind has found a way to keep Me out. It fills up the space and emptiness that is needed to hear Me. It fills up with thoughts and fears of future and past. People do not even think for a moment that the answers will come to them without thinking all the time."

I was so joyful to hear the voice once again! I spoke with Him about how people think and how they think they know what other people think. I asked God to tell me about truth. All my life, I had been plagued with not understanding why people do and say what they do. I had always thought there was something wrong with me because many reactions of others to what I said and did came to me as a surprise. So I asked God, "What is truth?"

God replied, "The most simple of all things, dear girl: truth is."

I stopped for a moment and looked around. The tree under which I sat *was*. The white-capped lake I could see across from me *was*. The sky and the clouds *were*. Everything I could see *was*. Simply put, the truth was right in front of me in that present moment; it *was*.

I asked the voice to explain more about truth.

"The truth changes from each set of eyes that see it and each location from which it can be seen. It changes with the seasons and as the light changes in the sky. It is always changing as your perception and other variables change it. Truth is now. Now is the only reality. Truth is."

When I asked the voice how I might know the truth when I am speaking with someone and whether or not I could know how to respond based upon what the person told me at that time, I had my greatest revelation.

God told me that no one else in this world has my very same piece of truth. He spoke of how each one of us has a different past, with different experiences and life situations, and He spoke of how we see the world differently because of our past experiences and situations. He told me that our perceptions contain variables and that there are infinite variables to every listener and every speaker. But of most importance, He told me that no other human being can have my piece of truth.

With that, my questions were answered instantly. I had so many questions about the world and why it was such a difficult place for people of different faiths, beliefs, and origins to live together in peace. That day, God spoke to me of harmony and of how peace could prevail. "It is quite simple," He said. "What is most important is to realize that who you perceive as your enemy really is someone seeing through a different pair of eyes, and what he sees is different. To know this is to honor another's piece of truth."

When that settled in, I sat for a while and wondered if God were only my piece of truth. Walking home from the lake that day, I felt both great affirmation and great doubt. The voice had been gone for so long, but at long last, I was hearing it again. He told me I had to be in my heart to hear it and that others could not hear it because they filled up space with thought. I wondered if His voice were real. I wondered if I might be living in a fantasy, and I wondered what was happening to me.

When I arrived home, the questions and thoughts became so intense that tears, once again, began to flow. My heart felt as though it were sinking deeper inside me, and reality was too sobering for the joy and passion I had felt in the garden. I cried myself to sleep that night, wondering if I were living in a land of make-believe or the real world. The balloon deflated, the cloud of joy sank to the ground, and the ship came into the harbor. I walked off with wobbly legs, shaky and seasick.

The next morning, I awoke to the sound of my cell phone by my bedside. I had overslept the sunrise because my mind had told me there was no need to wake up. I grabbed the phone and looked at the screen to see the number of the caller. It was a text message that said clearly in print: "Truth is."

I sprang up from bed, absolutely stunned! I had not spoken with anyone about this concept. It was my secret with the voice with whom I had been speaking the previous day. I became dizzy with disbelief at the prospect of the voice sending a text message! Then I remembered a letter I had written to a Buddhist teacher many months before, asking him what he felt about truth. I had set my cell phone to send me a text message if he were ever to reply, and since it had been many months before, I had forgotten. The message that he sent me was much longer than "Truth is," but that is all that would fit on the front of my cell phone. I knew it was more than a coincidence that this message had awakened me from sleep and that it had come the day after I had questioned my faith in the voice. I got up and looked out the window, finding the deer up against it sleeping soundly next to where my bed was placed.

That night, though a windy spring evening, the full moon rose in the eastern skies. I looked out the kitchen window from my favorite chair and saw its bright incandescence. Getting up slowly, I walked out the living room doors to pull down the umbrella rattling in the heavy winds. As I looked beyond the deck, I caught a small twinkling in the grass. It was a messenger and all his friends.

In the grass, four of my favorite deer friends had come to welcome me back to the world of the voice. The moon was low in the sky above them, its light shining brightly, representing God's grace in this wondrous majesty. I have never forgotten how God guided me through this leap of faith to help me believe He had heard me. Moreover, He wished to show me the way to live my life with His love, His joy, and His peace.

There are many leaps of faith that one takes on this journey, but the first one is the most important. The first leap is choosing God. For when we hear God's voice, our minds limit what we've heard and do not allow us to go to a place of peace and joy. It is never the mind's job to see what is right; it is the mind's job to teach us what it knows and keep us out of danger, thereby restricting us from a place of infinite possibility. Our minds cannot tell us of what they do not know, and God is not within our minds. It is up to our hearts to take the leap of faith and believe.

CHAPTER 8

The Journey of Inverse Thinking

I journeyed on through the seasons, and my conversations with God became longer and felt deeper to me. I learned to wake up with the sunrise, no matter the season, and be with that present moment. Then I watched the painting that God created on our skies, as it was soon gone to the clouds or the sunshine. One never knows what one never sees. My routine was not to be fooled with, and when I was lax in following through, I felt anxiety in place of peace and regret in place of awareness. Right after the sunrise, I pulled out a journal and spent time recording my fears and thoughts. Then I observed the present and listened to the silence in the house. Soon, the conversations with God naturally followed, and I learned how to record them in my journal. What began as one page of dialogue, months later, became pages and pages of teachings to which my questions to God would lead.

I was filled with many questions about leaps of faith, and I found that when I was most filled with thought, God's voice was most elusive to my ears. By then, I had come to recognize that I could not have a conversation with the voice when I was stressed, thinking, or trying to solve a problem—unless I had the consciousness to ask the question from my heart. Putting this together took many months; it occurred to me in bits and pieces and occasional revelations. When I was within my heart, this journey was one of epiphanies and major shifts in paradigm. The way I had thought all my life had to be replaced with this new way that gave me such peace and joy. My heart jumped out of my chest with passion when I was with God!

I came to realize there are many leaps of faith when experiencing God. What I learned was unlike what I had been taught in religious school or had discussed in conversations about religion. Every step toward God was a step away from my mind and a step toward the emptiness and an appreciation of the creation that happens there.

One morning, I talked with God about this and about how I felt so unaligned with Him when I had a lot about which to think. The obstacles that my mind saw were really changes in terrain that my heart felt, and if I viewed these situations from a place within my heart, a door of wisdom opened up to me. Sometimes when I was too tired to think, it was a good thing, for my heart did not require my body's energy to give me the wisdom I needed.

"Do you see how it happens?" God asked me one fine morning.

"I am beginning to," I replied.

"Do you doubt it?" the voice continued.

"When I am unaligned, I doubt everything we do together."

"This is how you know if you are unaligned: you can no longer feel your faith in Me," God said.

Suddenly, an awareness dawned on me. "The word *faith* is a curious one. Most use it to describe religious beliefs, but faith is really an action."

"Yes, it is. It is always there, but most do not use it, and most do not ever go this deep unless they are forced into surrender or they feel there is no other choice. Faith is only about the knowing that I am at the center. Many fear going that deep and losing the 'world,' but one must go that deep to find Me. That loss is so pivotal to spiritual change," God said.

"I understand now," I said. "So it's not building faith; it's uncovering faith?"

"Yes, Frannie. You have uncovered Me in the center."

"Why do we test faith, God?"

"Actually, you think I test faith. I do not. I just put it there. I only help you to uncover it—if you have space enough in your life to listen."

Our conversation continued, and with time, more and more of God's wisdom came to me from deep within my heart. I realized that God is elusive when we are in our minds, in the *thinking* mode. The way God appears to us in life is somewhat like an optical illusion. We can see an optical illusion one way or another, but not both ways at once. With God, it works the same way. If we are filled with thoughts and no space, we will have only thoughts and no space. If we allow the emptiness and listen to the silence, then God will come forth into our consciousness and show us the way.

It is merely a journey of inverse thinking. What we have been doing does not work. In fact, it is the opposite—what we have not done—that works. We think that life has to be complicated because the mind likes complex thought; that helps it stay in control. In truth, it is the very simple that is the way to God—not the complex. The simplest answers and the most heartfelt yearnings are the ways God calls to us in our lives. We mistake this longing for wanting and needing, because we are conditioned to look outside of ourselves for what is inside of us. God is inside our longing. It's really as simple as that.

When I was a child, I loved quiet, rainy days when I could be soulful and heartfelt. Those days blanketed me in a peace no other time could give me. Now, looking back, I can see why: There was nothing to do but just *be* on days like those. They were days of space. Sitting and writing and observing were all I could do on a soul day. What I felt at that time was God pulling me closer, and I now recognize those feelings as the peace and love of God. I wonder if that is how it is with most human beings in the world. Do they have soul days that they ignore or try to fill up with busywork so they can account for the time they spent sitting? Isn't it that most of the world needs to show something they produced in order to feel as though a day were well spent?

While we are producing and keeping busy, God sits in the center of our being, waiting for us to come deeper into our hearts and call to Him. Why is it that we only call to Him when we are suffering, as I did? Perhaps, in those times, the mind has let us down, and there is nowhere to hide except in God's arms.

God is elusive to the thinking mind, but if we take the time and space to go deeper inside, we will find Him right where he always was—deep in the middle of our hearts. When we finally realize that all the looking and seeking has taken us back to our true Selves, we realize how very weary all this thinking has made us and how peaceful it is finally to be home.

CHAPTER 9

The Sacred Beauty of God's Majesty

Although the life I was living was one of beauty, life situations continued while on this journey, and the terrain on my path became rough fairly often. Sometimes it had to do with medications that controlled my illness, and other times, financial challenges occurred since I did not have the endurance to work at all at the time. Bills were catching up with us from my hospitalizations and dealing with four people's needs. At times, it was difficult to stay centered on my journey when there were calculations to make and a financial picture to address. One day, in looking at the figures, I realized it would be difficult to keep our home if things remained as they were. We would have to come up with a solution or put it on the market and find something we could afford on one income.

I loved my home. I loved the wildlife that knew where we lived and the places within it where I had found solace. It was a sad notion to be thinking of selling it as a result of fallout from those seventeen years of illness. I struggled with the idea and had many conversations with God about it. It really came down to a wish to keep it—a very, very strong wish.

One day I was sitting in my back yard under the crab apple tree, just as it was about to flower. The fragrance of its soon-to-be blossoms was amazing, and I recorded in my journal a conversation with God about the likelihood of losing our home. It was there that God shared with me the difference between wants and wishes.

"God, can you tell me if we will lose our home? I worry so, as this is the place where I have heard You and felt You in my heart. I wish to stay here forever."

"Dear Frannie, do you want to stay in your house, or is this something you wish?" God asked.

"Oh, it's a huge wish of mine to never leave the place where I have found such peace, as just entering the doorway makes me smile."

"Frannie, do you know the difference between a want and a wish?" God asked.

"I am unsure of where You are going with this, but I will venture a guess that wants are not as good as wishes. This feels more like a wish to me than just wanting something."

"You always get what you wish for, dear girl," God said.

"Please tell me more," I asked in complete curiosity.

"Wishes, My dear, come from within your heart. They are part of your destiny to bring you closer to Me. Wants are things you desire from outside of you that have nothing to do with our path together."

I was surprised by this answer since I never had been aware of a difference, but when I felt my heart pull at me, I could see the difference in the yearning. A want was a pulling away from God. A wish was a pulling from God.

I asked more questions that day, and I felt a calm about my home. It was time for another leap of faith, and I surrendered the situation to God. With time, a solution came to us that felt as though it fell from the sky because it was so very random and unexpected. I took a big jump forward, with the knowing that, if I remain open and do not always try to look for answers, sometimes the answers will simply come to me as a gift.

I was not always peaceful in the time before the answer came. We all tend to go back to comfortable patterns during times of challenge, with the illusion that we are controlling things that way. We think that if we do the same things all the time, then we will create a good and familiar outcome. On many occasions, I caught myself falling back into these old mind traps—until God told me about the gifts.

One July morning, I woke up before dawn to the pitter-patter of little feet on the deck. There in front of my eyes in the screen window were four little raccoon babies with the most beauty-filled faces, cute as can be. I rubbed my eyes and remembered that this was the beginning of the month of babies, and I had four little gifts in front of me to start my day.

God had told me about the gifts many times. He told me that the secret to the journey is to look for them and find joy in them. Each and every day, the gifts can be infinite in number, but how many do we see? God told me that gifts were things within my awareness that were very simple. They were things I would not see ordinarily, but because I was looking from a place of space, I would see them. I learned to see each day through the space of presence; the gifts in front of me were things I simply had passed over before. With our minds so filled, we miss them although they are right in front of us: the hawk flying over our car while we drive, the rainbow that appears within our view, the spectacular flower that grows in the cracks of a concrete walk. All of these are gifts. They are meant to be seen, but with our busy minds, we are lucky if we even notice they exist.

I often remember the essence of something about which the Sufi poet Rumi spoke eight hundred years ago. He taught that when someone gives us something, our hearts should rest within the heart of the giver rather than in the value of the gift.

The Giver is God. The One who is in the essence of every gift is the Creator. We work without feeling the givens, and we sleep without ever knowing one gift was given to us. God is elusive to our minds, and so are His gifts. To live our lives with meaning and purpose, we must uncover the pull inside these gifts. This is the deepest longing inside our hearts, and we must have the space and emptiness to embrace it.

The next morning, I was awakened by a scared fawn crying for its mother as it ran through the yard. Its piercing call touched my heart with sadness. I knew well the feelings of abandonment and loneliness. The fawn stopped abruptly, and several minutes later, I saw its mom nursing it in front of my door. I felt the fawn's feelings. I knew it was lost, and I connected with it. Connecting with another life is our greatest gift of all.

Looking carefully at the life I was given, I learned to see my walks through nature and connection to all living things as an adventure of infinite possibilities. Anything could happen. Each day, I awoke to hear the birds chirping, to enjoy breakfast with the deer family, and to greet the morning red fox—always making contact with the light within their eyes. In silence, I watched the sunrise each day with the crows. A new sense of wonder filled me as I admired a mural being painted by a God who spoke only in the present moment. Some days, the picture was so touching that I sat in amazement as colors I had never seen before flowed through the vast space of the skies, only to disappear as quickly as they came. After the silence of this wondrous observance, the crows chatted passionately and flew off in different directions. I walked off in mine, toward the lake, where more beauty would astound me.

If I left my home early enough in the morning quiet, I would come upon the blue heron that sat solitarily on the rock-covered bank and stared across the lake. He glanced off into the distance as I tried to sense what he was all about. He appeared spindly and delicate, with a certain pride that reminded me of the way trees stand so tall in gusty winds. I felt his deep awareness of my footsteps as I approached. During my walk each day, he let me come closer to admire the detail on his small face, and I watched as he gathered his breakfast from between tiny white pebbles by the lake. He stood with legs of twigs, eyes never leaving me as I stepped forward on my journey with God.

When I returned home from my walks through the majesty, I journaled each gift I remembered. During those times, I had lengthier conversations with God, and I noted answers to questions and lessons He was trying to teach me. Conversations were deeper. I was learning about the creations of life that were in front of me, and the feelings that they brought to me taught me more about the deepest part of my Self.

Over time, I learned to see gifts as easily as I had once seen problems. Becoming automatic with this new insight, I felt a new feeling of joy that turned into a lasting blanket of peace. Surrender was an adventure in living life one moment at a time. I was aware of things I had been unable to see in my life before.

Sitting on a warm rock bench in the meditation garden, autumn leaves rained down on me from the oak trees. I awoke to my surroundings as if my heart were walking into color. A closer look at three leaves by my feet revealed that they were not leaves at all. Like a majestic moment in a fairy tale, the leaves from the ground gracefully flew into the air and surrounded me before rising into sky as a beautiful cloud of yellow monarch butterflies!

As I sat completely mesmerized by all the butterflies, one landed on my shoulder, as though I were a flower, and another settled on the sidewalk in front of me, opening his wings to show me his inner beauty.

God said, "You must open up to show your beauty. It's inside."

We spoke of how easily a butterfly does this and how hard a simple act like this is for a human being.

As I got up and walked on, within every pile of leaves, I found a gift of several butterflies. My heart jumped out of my chest with excitement. Surrounded by golden colors on the wings of beauty, I felt bathed in God's majesty. I walked through the garden, radiant with reverence for the life I was given but tempered by knowing how limited my life had been before the illness. I thought that having an illness had imprisoned me, but I was learning how the bars had always been there—all the days of my life!

The blue heron and I became good friends, and over time, God taught me how to feel His peace before I entered the blue heron's space. The heron allowed me to pass by him each day and share the light in our eyes for small moments of mutual connection. This was God's world, not man's world, and neither man's rules nor science mattered here. All that matters is sensing the infinite within one's Self and acknowledging without expectations.

In autumn, God and I spoke of the connection from one living soul to another, and God told me that we all connect through the God center within our hearts. That day, I went out and felt the leaves on trees and the flowers, and I felt the wings of the butterflies flutter to their peaceful rhythm. I continued along my journey, moving forward one step at a time. Each day brought new gifts, and some days, there were so many that I had to rest under the pine trees to allow my heart to expand in such joy.

Over time, my mind lost its ability to rock my world. There were too many gifts to label life situations as problems anymore. The present moment was all that mattered to my heart. Life situations were things to deal with, but they did not deter me from the true meaning of living. To me, the sky signified my life, and though clouds passed through my view from time to time, there was always a bright sun underneath them. I knew this in every present moment of each day. Realizing that life is different from problems—and that problems come and go through life—changed my perspective and helped me see the gifts as the most important part of my journey.

CHAPTER 10

You Always Get What You Wish For

On a cool autumn day, my favorite deer friend's youngest son walked into my yard with one of his small antlers hanging by a thread and the other knocked hard to the side. It was November, mating season, or rutting season as we call it in Colorado, when the young male deer are taught by the elders how to use their antlers to practice fighting with each other. To watch them doing this is always entertaining as they run about the yard, jumping like overgrown rabbits and going after each other with their antlers. There are bound to be injuries, and many times, one or both deer lose their antlers.

Satara, as I named him, often walked through our neighborhood perusing the bushes for berries on which to snack. I learned to recognize him by the size of his antlers and a large scar on his right thigh. When I called Satara by name, he usually responded by walking toward me. He and I had a very gentle relationship, and I often found him in the church garden where I would call his name. At times, he would come and stand beside me. The fact that his height equaled my five feet two inches made this closeness a little unnerving. I wondered if his wild ways might suddenly appear, but the truth was that Satara seemed taken with me, as I was with him.

On that autumn day, I could see that Satara's antlers were soon to be history. I walked outside and noticed that there were bleeding and open wounds upon his head. Standing in piles of golden leaves, I spoke to him gently. Seeing the light shining in his eyes, I felt him make hard and long contact with mine. For many moments, I felt he knew my heart, and I wished to stand there with him forever. There is nothing greater than the love one feels when making contact with a wild one, one whose heart is connected in God, for there is a knowing that only God could make this so. I stood there and spoke gently to my young friend about his antlers.

"Satara, I see you are hurting so much because of your antlers. You have lost your power among the men of your kind, yet I know you have such great power within your heart. Use it. Be His peace, and He will protect you."

My friend stared back at me, and the light in his eyes touched mine. As he moved closer, I could see his breath go in and out of his long, graceful nose which was wet and alive.

"Satara, please leave your antlers here with me, and I will keep them safe. I will cherish them because I know how much they have meant to you."

For many long minutes, Satara stood by me as we gazed into each other's eyes. I knew the pain he was suffering from the blow of his rutting was more than just physical; losing his antlers would make him weaker in his brothers' eyes. Weakness was something he already felt because he had always limped. His right leg had been broken when he injured his thigh as a young fawn. I felt Satara's weakness, and he felt mine. For many moments, I felt the compassion I had been asking God to teach me.

The winds picked up from the north, and the leaves blew swiftly. It was getting cold outside, signaling an impending fall snow. Needing a sweater to fend off the chill, I said goodnight to Satara and walked into the house, leaving him in the middle of my garden with his head gazing up at the sky.

The sun went down beneath our purple mountains, and the sky slowly changed from blue to gray. Winds blew fiercely, forcing Satara to stay in my yard all night. In his presence, I felt God's love. Leaves were strewn everywhere—from the garden, to the fence, to our deck, and to our back door. The winds blew loudly all night long.

In the early morning, I awoke to God's voice asking me to go into the yard and look deep into the leaves. I walked several feet backward and forward, and then I felt it—something hard and sharp under the leaves by my feet. Bending over and brushing off the dirt, I found one of Satara's antlers amidst the leaves. It had two points, like fingers making a peace sign or a victory sign—God's sign for peace, Satara's sign for love. I walked several feet forward, and there on top of the rocks lay the other antler, in a similar peace sign fashion. I stood there, both in disbelief and with great faith, with a knowing that Satara was God's gift to me, and his antlers were now mine to keep safe forever. I heard God's words—softly at first, but then quite lovingly. "Frannie Rose, sweet Frannie Rose, you always get what you wish for."

I was astounded that my wish for Satara's antlers would be granted by God and amazed at the love of this Creator toward His creation. It became clear to me that other creatures on our earth have this same connection with Him, and I realized we take for granted that their souls are not as important as ours. Surely, I learned, we are all connected through Him at the center, and if we wish for something from deep within our hearts, we will always get what we wish for.

CHAPTER 11

Parables, Metaphors, and Synchronicities

One early autumn day when I was feeling a little blue, I sat on a stone bench underneath a strong, wide-limbed oak tree. In its majesty, the tree was losing its leaves, shedding the old to make room for the new. I saw more leaves on the ground than on the branches. The leaves lay in piles beside me, glowing in their colors of the season. Barren, the tree branches seemed naked and lonely. Looking up into the tree's branches, I felt its grace and beauty. The piles on the ground were airy, inviting, old leaves like shells that once held such life inside. As they aged, they celebrated by bursting into color. Each leaf fell slowly on its own special journey to the ground.

I sat among the leaves on a bench just a little higher off the ground than they were. As my heart opened to the present moment and I connected with the beauty around me, I felt an incredible freedom and wonder, but it soon turned to conflict. Becoming aware that I felt little concern about outcomes and the future, I feared becoming disconnected from man's world. I had no fears about death. There was acceptance where I once had felt fear. Talking with God that morning, he explained this natural progression.

"God, please tell me about life and death. These leaves are so beautiful. It's a shame they had to die."

"Frannie Rose, death is not an ending. Your body's death is a new beginning for the life of the soul. The life you are living now is like a tunnel the soul journeys through. And when a body dies, the soul travels on through the tunnel to a new day, a new way with Me."

"God, why do the leaves become so beautiful before they die?"

His answer was heartfelt. "Frannie Rose, they blossom into color because they are joyous for having journeyed through a world they thought was real, only to find a deeper place where they may be with Me."

What a wonderful story of endings that become beginnings! What a wonderful way to look at things! Gazing up at the trees, I saw some leaves that remained green, hanging tightly to their branches. I felt quite curious about those.

"Frannie Rose, there are some leaves that are fearful of death and what lies ahead. They hold tightly to life, ignoring the truth. These old, drained leaves have grown tired and weak, tightly grasping a branch all winter while barely holding on through the snow and cold, until finally a strong, swift wind blows them off the branches and takes them to where they belong, closer to Me."

Later that fall, when I came again to sit on the rock bench in the church garden, the leaves were gone. The sun warmed the sidewalk in front of me. In my contemplation, I looked down and saw a curious sight. An ant was walking down the sidewalk toward the grass, and it was carrying a large dead beetle.

Fascinated by the strength of the ant, and thinking that he was lucky to have found dinner, I watched it carefully. It did not appear to be struggling as it carried the beetle to the edge of the grass. When the ant arrived at its destination, it stopped suddenly. I watched the dead beetle come to life and walk into the grass! Stupefied, I asked God about this.

"How could that be, God? How is this happening? What am I missing?"

God answered me gently and lovingly. "What do you think happened, Frannie Rose?"

"I thought the beetle somehow recovered," I answered, bewildered. "He must have become really frightened when he realized he was in an ant's grasp."

"Is this what your mind is telling you, Frannie Rose? Does your heart say anything?"

"My heart felt so bad for the beetle, dear God."

"Frannie Rose, the ant and the beetle were friends. Yes, they were friends! The human mind does not believe that all beings have souls. All beings do have souls. The human mind says that their brains are too small. Their brains are large and complex enough to feel. The beetle had fears about crossing the concrete. The ant was helping him to the other side. It is what human beings feel within their own hearts. You call it compassion."

"Are you telling me ants have compassion, dear God? The way they live and how I have been taught they are does not speak to this."

"Human beings do not know what goes on in another creature's soul, Frannie Rose. They assume so much. They think what their minds tell them is the only truth. Your mind only tells you what other minds have taught it, Frannie Rose. It is only a wounded human being who cannot feel compassion. Most of my beings can."

Another metaphor had been given to me. How blessed I felt that I could know from my Creator about His creation. I was learning so much about the gentleness of God. My walk home that day was full of joy and love for all God's creatures. It was a compassionate universe He created.

The journey through the majestic greenery continued as green-carpeted seasons changed into wondrous, sugarcoated seasons. The snowflakes held a special place in my heart during winter as I observed their distinct personalities while they managed through the winds of a storm. Glued to the window on the days I could not walk, I watched them carefully and saw that some snowflakes flew through the skies as though they had been set free to explore every air current. Others repositioned themselves for the best aerodynamics to lengthen their journey straight down at high speeds toward the ground. I wondered about those daring enough to take the straight path downward, without the beauty of the view but with such intense speed. My heart felt excitement as snowflakes were pulled toward the ground. Lost in their movement, I imagined they were riding a wave in the air. Each snowflake had a different path, unique to its size and shape. Just as they say no two snowflakes are exactly the same, neither are their paths from the clouds to the earth.

When our lives begin to feel more of a gift than a problem, even when we meet with adversity, we need simply sit in front of a window to know a way of living that is full of beauty and great peace. As I sat there during the snowstorms, God taught me more about such ways by the movement of each snowflake. A new way of being was opening from a depth inside my heart to which I had never before felt so connected. Every day became a soul day, and my conscious task was to find the gifts and share their beauty with God.

On our walks together, God taught me to look for metaphors that would make me more aware of lessons in the life around me. Things that happened on my way contained a simple symbolism I could not brush off, and I realized that most humans tend to ignore this. Happenings as simple as walking into a tree branch were symbolic of a lesson I needed to learn. The simple tree branch was God's way of saying, "Wake up!" Later, I learned that if I did not heed the call to do so, I soon would be in a dangerous position, crossing streets unconsciously.

Some mornings, the simple wake-up call was God gently showing me the way. Once warned, I learned to focus on what I saw, heard, and felt, enough for me to see subtler gifts that I might not have seen otherwise. The metaphors became more meaningful as I ventured deeper into God's teachings. God spoke to me of the ripples on the lake and what He wished me to do with His teachings when He felt I was ready. I had no idea about the specifics, but my heart nearly jumped out of my chest when He spoke of it. I observed my mind trying to leave the present and bolt ahead with the task to become ready for God. However, I ignored its need to live for the future; instead, I allowed myself the beauty of the present moment.

From reading, I knew that many spiritual students had teachers, but I knew no human being with whom I could speak about what had happened to me. Feeling far from organized religion, I desired to read ancient texts from all religions. Although I never had looked at them before, a common thread tied them together when read for the essential message within each. There were elements within all these readings that I experienced from such a deep place that I felt their truth. They were each like pieces of a pie, touching at the center, and the center was God. I learned that it is God we all have in common and God who brings us together. For a while, I was partial to the Buddhist writings because they seemed to speak of something close to what I was feeling, but as time passed, I saw the truth in all religions. I saw God in the center.

Afterward, I had a serious heart-to-heart with God, feeling once again that I needed the human contact of a teacher. God told me that religion is merely a vehicle to Him, but not the end result. He mentioned that it was the job of religion to bring us to Him, but where we take it from there is up to *We*—God and each of us. We spoke about churches, retreat settings, meditation, and other religious practices, and I asked Him two important questions: Did I need a church? Did I need a teacher?

"God, all religions have disciplines and structure that are unique to them. Please tell me why. Why do they need these special prayers and ways to worship You?"

"Dear, dear Frannie, prayers and worship are not necessary to find Me, as you have found. All that is needed is the emptiness to be with Me. I am with each human being all the time in every aspect of their hearts. Perhaps if they listened to their hearts, they would know this, but they do not. Church has become the place where they are closer to their hearts for a limited period of time."

"But, God, why are they closest to their hearts in church?"

"It is the one time in their week when they take time out of their busy schedules to try to connect with Me. It's the one time they create space and emptiness."

"I have learned to find You in the freedom and the beauty of my own heart. In church and temple, people are saying what the words in the books tell them to say. Please tell me, how can we get closer to our hearts that way?"

"Devoting the time and space to our connection is what brings a human being to Me. I am not in the space that is filled with another's words. I am in the peace of a present moment and the openness of one's heart. Churches, temples, and religious traditions are structure. Their initial intention was to keep Me in. But because I am infinite and their walls are finite, in many, they have kept Me out."

I felt deeply about what God told me, and in all the religious traditions with which I was familiar, people were told what to see and what to read. They spoke the words of another rather than speaking the feelings of their own hearts. I realized why I never had been able to find solace within a religious service, and yet, there was so much

God within the space of a temple or a church. I asked God more about why this is.

"God, it is within the sacred space of a church or a temple that people wish to come and pray. A church or temple is a limited space; so when is there beauty in doing that?"

"It is not physical space that limits Me, dear Frannie; it is the space within one's mind. Hearing another's words fills up one's mind, weighing it heavily upon the heart. Your connection with Me is from within your heart. If one's mind is filled with words he is being told to say, then the feelings within the heart become elusive. I am elusive to your mind, dear Frannie, and I can be found only within your heart."

I realized how seldom we take heart time in our society today. It is all about production, achievement, and future. One must have something to show for the work he did, or a mind considers that day a waste of time. I have had so many soul days on this journey, and I realized that in the world from which I came, a soul day has no meaning. The soul can be found only in a now moment, and present moments are filled up with have tos, need tos, and, only rarely, heartfelt moments.

There was great truth in what God told me that day: Religion has become big business, with rituals, prayers, and financial agreements to add to the already endless structure. From the moment one enters a church or a sanctuary, the program is written for him. As I looked at the depth of my journey with God, I realized that my relationship with God was dependent upon the emptiness within me, not a program filled with words to say and repeat. I saw the discrepancies between the emptiness that is needed for an experience of God and the structure that is seen in religious practices today.

This new lesson did not answer my question about having a teacher, and so I asked God again about this. "God, do I need a teacher in order to learn from this very beautiful journey with You?"

"My dear Frannie, if you wish to find a teacher, find one. But you know in your heart that I have always been your teacher."

I felt a strong need to find someone who would understand what I was experiencing. I wished to talk with a human being about this journey and to know of others who might have walked this path. Deciding to make an appointment with a priest I knew seemed to be the next step. I went to the appointment confused about how to explain my experience, and I left the appointment feeling no connection, no "click." The priest called my story an experience of "presence," warning me to keep my feet on the ground. He sat very seriously, watching me closely, without any heart connection to this wondrous story. He appeared to come from a place of judgment rather than a place of God or heart.

At that crucial juncture on my journey, I realized what I felt was not experienced by most people in their lifetimes and that my experience was one unknown to many. Precious gifts from God had given me a renewed joy and gratitude for the alchemy that He had created within my life. In my heart, I realized that where I was going was not something that most people's minds would allow them to understand. I cautiously stepped closer to God, weighing carefully what had happened to me against the possible harm that could be done; I weighed heart and mind. Before surrendering to God, life had been meaningless and without purpose. Now I was more functional in the world, and it was obvious that my joy and peace had increased manifold. The rest of what my mind told me was a bunch of speculation. After all, my mind knew nothing about what I was experiencing, so why would I try to evaluate this situation from a level of mind?

What I learned about structured religion became priceless to me, and what God taught me about the emptiness was the lesson I used to frame my life. I rearranged the space as the ultimate priority, and tasks that had to be done I did in short segments early in the day. Instead of making the tasks the focus, I made the space the focus. For as I recovered from this illness, and the years passed in the greenery, space became the focus and the life situations were only happenings within the space. This was the inverse of what I had done before God began teaching me. For most of my life, I had viewed space as something to fill. The space God taught me to see as my life is the same space from where my breath comes and in which God creates.

Early one morning, I walked over the bridge and asked God if I might be able to find a kindred soul with whom to discuss my journey. "God, is there anyone out there who would understand what we are doing together?"

"Frannie, there is someone moving toward you as we speak, as the hawk moves toward you in the sky. When you are ready, this someone will come to you."

I looked up at the sky, and flying above me was a red-tailed hawk. "How will one come to me?" I asked, wanting to know more about the future.

"One will come in the most unpredictable way."

CHAPTER 12

When the Teacher Is Ready

My days on the bridge became more frequent, and the beauty and metaphors continued. Each day, I walked down the grass, onto the sidewalks, and over the street to the lake. My heart would slow as I listened to God through this walk, and He taught me how to breathe to slow down my heart. By the time I trekked to the bridge and stood over the lake looking at the mountains, my mind was empty, and my heart was open. It was there that God had spoken to me of teaching others. He had said to me, rather simply, "Teach them to hear Me."

I wondered how I would go about doing that as I had no credentials and no background in theology or religion. I took this seriously, but I put it in the back of my mind, forgetting about it for a short while.

Many months passed, and I forgot about this person moving toward me. My journey continued to deepen, and teachings came from God every day. My husband wished for me to talk with a nun he had met at a company retreat, for he perceived that she was very spiritual. I did not wish to allow others to choose the people with whom I spoke, and because of this resistance, I waited almost six months before contacting this nun via e-mail. Her secretary arranged a date and time for her to see me. I wasn't sure what I was going to say to her, but I felt I would know within that present moment.

I walked into her office, and she sat behind a table with a stern look on her face. I turned away from her at first, but when I finally looked up into her eyes, they were the most radiant blue I had ever seen, and they were sparkling. I knew that sparkle from others who were important to my journey. I told her the story of my journey, and she listened deeply. Then, almost involuntarily, I felt my heart jumping to ask her a question that leaped out of my chest. "Sister Nancy, have you ever heard God's voice?"

She looked away quickly, and then, as if with regret, she focused deeply on my face. "No, my dear girl, I am sad to say, I have not."

Again, impulsively bursting from the depth of my heart, the words jumped out of my mouth before I could hold them in. "Sister Nancy, would you like me to teach you?"

Her eyes opened wide as a child's, her face graced with wonder, and I could feel the warmth from the flush in her cheeks. Could this be a dream come true for her? I didn't know, but I felt aligned, as though I had just found a very big breadcrumb from God.

She replied affirmatively, and we arranged a date and time for her to come to my home and sit with me. Wondering how I would be able to do this, I checked with God about what had happened.

"A breadcrumb, dear Frannie, a breadcrumb. You picked it up and put it into your heart. This is the beginning of the path you wish for and I wish for you."

"But, God, what path? How do you know this?" I asked Him to explain.

"Remember the feeling, dear girl. Remember the way your heart felt when you asked her. This is how it happens, without thinking or dancing carefully around the words. It leaps out from your heart as a longing, just as I jumped out from your heart that beautiful day when you first heard My voice."

I always had been taught that one should think before speaking, and this was a new way of being. It was as if my heart knew the words although my mind did not know of the wish. It seemed perfectly natural, not deliberate like decisions and choices I had made before in my life. It was an innate sort of flow; as water flows from an elevated place to a lower place, so did my feelings flow from a deeper place within me. God had led me to Sister Nancy with the breadcrumbs of synchronicities that had occurred. I later found out that Sister Nancy had not been seeing new people six months prior, when my husband had wanted me to see her. Only recently had she opened her schedule to people who called her from outside the hospital system within which she worked.

Even later, I learned that Sister Nancy had thought I was responding to a newspaper article that had been written about a program in which she was involved. When I arrived and told her my story, it was as if I had fallen from the sky; the meeting was so out of context to her expectation. When reminiscing about how we met, we realized it was a gift for both of us as we journeyed onward together.

I had come to her to find a teacher to help guide me on this journey. This turn of events was so unexpected as I walked out of the nun's office as the teacher with a new student. I had become the teacher for whom I had been searching all along.

On the way home, I spoke with God, asking if this event were something He had wished for me. "God, I walked in looking for a human being to share our journey with, and somehow I became her teacher. How did this happen?"

"We spoke of this several months ago, dear Frannie, while you were walking on the bridge. Do you remember?"

Thinking back, I recalled having to shut off my mind, as my eagerness to meet this individual tempted me to jump into the future from the peace of that present moment. "I do remember now. Is this the person You spoke of? Am I to share my journey with her?"

God answered me gently, "Your journey will parallel her journey in many ways, dear Frannie, and what you give to her will bring her to where her heart has always wished to be—with Me."

Excitement followed me home that evening as wondrous hope had been uncovered in those moments within Sister Nancy's office. I sensed an unseen purpose and a chance to serve God in a way that I never had imagined possible. I was going to use the gift given to me by God to do something beautiful for another soul. Already the message of this journey had begun to bear fruit.

These meetings with Sister Nancy uncovered many interesting parallels. Each lesson we sat through together yielded teachings for her and concurrent messages for me. Having the role of the teacher was purely an egoist title, as both the teacher's journey and the student's journey flow together in beautiful ways, each fulfilling a purpose for the other. We were both teachers, and Sister Nancy taught me more about my own ego than I ever had learned before. By watching my reactions to her struggles, I could feel my own heart rise up higher than it had walking alone over the bridge. I felt compassion and a deeper love than I ever had felt for a friend before, as our relationship was based upon our deepest hunger, God.

I learned in my work with her that God created both of us and God connected both of us.

Our journey together began with a miracle, and the miracles never ceased as long as we were together. She came to my home from a city north of me and traveled more than 140 miles for our teachings. When she arrived, we would sit in stillness together with our focus on our hearts. Within minutes, the animals came into my yard—the deer, the birds, cats, and a beautiful red fox.

The red fox became our companion during these sessions together. There were times in the midafternoon when I was astounded at his curiosity about us. He came up to my sliding glass door and lay comfortably on a lounge chair. Often, he stayed the whole three hours we were together, lying out on the deck by the window, looking in and listening carefully to our hearts. I was able to capture him on camera many times, for I surely would not believe it unless I could see a picture of it. Our minds are funny that way; looking back, sometimes we tend to think our imaginations ran wild. In this case, it was a wild animal, sure as could be, quietly and peacefully there through our lesson, and as Sister Nancy and I got up to end our time, the fox walked off merrily on his way. We knew he had gotten an earful as he pranced off, enlightened, to his next destination. He would always stay the whole time we were together—a metaphor that God was connecting with us both.

There was a time when I put three glasses of water out on the table—one for Sister Nancy, one for me, and one for God. By the time our session was over, God's glass was half full. Sister Nancy and I were astonished, and we spoke about the synchronicity of this occurrence. Human minds will come up with any possible reason they know of to explain away something of such magnitude, but with two of us there, we had to be confronted with the real truth: we did not know why it happened. It was just as possible that it could have been God who drank the water as any other possibility our minds could conjure. It was then that I was taught to find the faith to adopt the attitude "prove it isn't so."

More of these synchronous gifts occurred as we met more frequently together, and over time, Sister Nancy began to hear God's voice. She, too, was journaling her conversations with God as wisdom was sprinkled on her life. Our friendship blossomed from one of student and teacher to one of heart. Our connection became one of great strength and purpose, as we grounded one another when we needed grounding and flew when we wished to fly.

Though my life became richer with this student and friend, it was not filled up, and my journey continued to grow deeper. As I learned to function from a place of space, I had very few appointments and was at home most days, deeply meditating. One summer day, a man rang the front doorbell, needing to change out our thermostat. He was a friendly man with a deep, jubilant voice, and when I looked into his eyes, I saw the sparkle of the blues of seas. Looking back, I realize he had the sparkle I had come to recognize as a person sent to me by God.

As he put in the thermostat, we talked about life and spirit and about God. I felt so much heart when speaking that I babbled a bit about spiritual journeys. He listened with great interest as I spoke some of his own truth. After he installed the thermostat, he told me about his church, which was around the corner from my home—the very churchyard where I heard God for the first time—and he asked me if I would consider teaching there. Astounded, as I had never considered myself a classroom teacher, I told him I would think about it. My heart jumped out of my chest once again with a deep wish to do this.

Another human being with the sparkle was one more breadcrumb on the path that God had chosen for me. I had no knowledge that he would be coming my way. All of what happened was a synchronous event that some might call simply a coincidence. I had come to learn that coincidences are the mind's way of ignoring God. From the time I left my bed, there were so many happenings, all of which held a purpose beyond the understanding of the human mind.

When such synchronous events happen, we rationalize them away with our minds, thinking there must be an explanation. After all, isn't there always an explanation for everything? Our minds tell us that if there isn't an explanation, it can't be real. But what if it isn't something a mind can understand? What if it's God showing us the way by dropping breadcrumbs to lead us to our destined paths?

On my walking meditations, I saw more and more of these gifts, synchronous events, and metaphors. On some days, I could find fifteen or twenty within my waking hours, as my level of awareness had become so keen. I could see things that most people passed by while they were talking on their cell phones, thinking about things they had to do, or otherwise filling up their space so much that there was no room to be aware of how God was leading them.

God communicates to us through these happenings that our minds debase to coincidence and happenstance. What at first gives our hearts great excitement our minds quickly dismiss as commonplace. When we feel with God and with other beings, we call these happenings into our presence, and when we are ready, the very best circumstances for us are offered to us. To experience these gifts, we must be aware enough to have the opening in our lives to see them. We create the space or the emptiness by living with patience, awareness, and flexibility, and by surrendering when we don't know what to do.

Walking into a miracle, I began to teach—small classes at first and then larger ones—and as I began to accumulate teachings from God, a deeper path opened up for me. I asked Him one day what He wished me to do with this, and His profound, yet simple answer brought chills to my heart.

"God, please tell me, what is it You most wish for me to teach these students?"

For a while, there was no answer, but one day, an answer came while I sat in front of the lake and listened to the geese. "Frannie, the human world has become a place of noise and problems. There is little time for solace within your storms of living. I call to many of you from time to time and place to place. I am never heard. Please teach them how to listen to Me and hear Me, for I have been speaking for such a long time."

My breath was taken by His words, and my eyes began to tear with His urgency. "You sound as if You are saddened by this, dear God. Please tell me what I must know in order to bring this message to our students."

"Human days are filled with things you do. Your silence is filled with thoughts from others. Your time with Me is filled with your words and words you read. There is no open space for My words. This time and age is a changing one, and situations on your planet are gaining momentum. I wish for you to listen to Me, as I wish to give you the answers. But you cannot hear Me from your busy mind. You can only hear Me from an open heart."

As the geese were speaking to one another loudly, I realized that His message was being heard by all around me. The trees began to blow loudly in the breeze, and I felt it blow my hair and skin. There was freedom in this wind, and as I felt my hair blowing with the breeze, I felt the change of which God spoke.

"Dear, dear God, I wish so much to help You to be heard. And this I will do because I am so grateful, and I realize what You say. There is so much chaos in the world right now, and I know chaos well from within my own life. You taught me how to cope with the unknown and not to fear it. You uncovered my hope and showed me the way to my heart. I will do the same for the students you have brought to me. Please give me always Your help."

"Frannie, the turmoil of the mind inside of each human being is manifested outside of you. Each human being is feeling inner chaos and confusion—I can feel this! There is very little time for reflection and no time to listen for Me. The result of this is external chaos, for the way of My world is from within to without. If individuals do not find peace within themselves, there will not be peace without. If individuals do not find compassion for themselves, they will never feel compassion for others. If individuals do not feel a love of life, enough to allow for meaning and purpose in their lives, they will not take part in the greater purpose of humankind. You may struggle with this, and this is why our work is so important. The human world is in turmoil as each human being looks upon others with judgment and blame. Judgment is not their task; it is Mine. Human beings rarely look within and ask Me to show them the way."

From the words I heard then, I knew the deeper truth. It did not matter how it was said, but it mattered very much that it was said. I could not walk away from that conversation carrying the same illusions with which I had begun.

"God, I will do as You ask. Isn't religion supposed to help take care of this?"

"They speak of Me, but they do not know Me. Many priests, rabbis, and pastors do not hear me. In churches and temples, they give people words to say and words to read, but there is not space to hear My voice. They speak at Me but without the space within their hearts to listen."

God asked me to teach these new students how to hear His voice from what I experienced, beginning with my own journey. I took these students to the place of wonder in walking meditations, seeing gifts and alchemy in their lives. When they were ready and knew how to see the world from God's beauty and with the keen eyes of a child, I taught them how to hear God speak to them.

Right before these deep brown eyes, the beauty-filled winds of change blew in, and these souls with weary minds became beaming hearts with God-centered awareness. I watched in amazement as God expanded inside them, forever transforming their lives. As seeds move to create strong sprouts, they break the shells in which they had learned to live, sprouting through the boundaries of the soil freely, to blossom from within to without.

Many seasons of sugarcoated mountaintops came and passed. I taught classes at the church and saw individuals struggling to find meaning and purpose in living. Through parallel lessons and teachings from God, I learned that within each of us are the seeds of love, hope, goodness, kindness, peace, joy, and generosity. Our society conditions us from the time of childhood to cover these with "more important" things, teaching us to bury our hearts with thought. Although our quests come in different-colored packages, our wish universally is still the same. God is our deepest hunger and our deepest longing. I learned that what was missing from our lives was missing for a reason, and with recognition of the empty space comes a new opportunity to surrender this sacred space to God. Emptiness does not have to mean "barren" or "lacking substance." Instead, it is an opening of potential or a field of infinite possibilities. Only our minds see it as lack. Our hearts see it as hope for something better, something wondrous, and something infinite: God.

CHAPTER 13

The Relationship and the Creed

My beautiful walks continued, and I looked forward to hearing from God each day. As days and months passed, I became excited and enlivened, jumping out of bed in the morning, sitting in front of the window, and watching the deep night light change into day. My routine consisted of being with silence and presence first thing each morning, creating space for God. It inspired me so to hear His voice each morning while I journaled my questions to Him and His responses back to me, carefully recording His words on paper. I awakened with great anticipation of what we would chat about together each day. I found that His reassuring answers and gentle words became the background of the picture of my day. Anything that happened to me after my time with God was seen from a place of grace instead of a place of inconvenience or disappointment. I realized there was a lesson in almost everything that happened in my life, and I was eager to learn from Him each day.

This journaling became sacred reflection time during which to go inward and learn about my true Self and the ego that often tried to block my relationship with God. I learned the only thing that comes between God and me is my ego. It manifests by judging me, comparing me to others, and limiting me. I learned that, with God, anything that happens is an opportunity. How much we tend to limit ourselves into doing what we always have done before! I found it easier to take risks in the direction of my heart and to be completely honest with people in a kind and loving way. God taught me all this by shining a light on my mind and on my heart. Journaling time became a time of deep learning and reflection.

What was most interesting to me was the relationship that had formed between God and me. It was as if it had always been this way, and I could no longer remember a time when God was not in my life. God explained it to me one day when I asked Him about it with curiosity.

"God, can you tell me why it feels as if I have always known You—even when I never really listened to You before in my life?"

"Frannie, you have always known Me. You are united with Me through all eternity. Our union is deep within your heart. It is your mind that walks away from this."

"I do not understand, God. Why would my mind walk away from something as spectacular and joyous as knowing You?"

"It has reigned so long, and it loves the control you think you have over your life. The truth is the inverse; there is no control. Your mind limits you to give you fewer options and fewer choices for it to think about—creating comfort as you think you know what to expect in any situation. But the truth, dear Frannie, is My reality, a greater reality than your mind can fathom. The possibilities I give you are endless. You have choices and freedom with Me that the mind cannot give you, and because the outcome is Mine, the possibilities far surpass anything your mind can anticipate."

"So you are telling me that the mind comes between You and me and restricts Your infinite possibilities?"

"It does so by becoming so heavy that you no longer feel your heart."

I thought about this, and felt about it, and realized that our society today has lost sight of the heart. We have become desensitized by rules, government, media, and big businesses. Even within my own healthcare, it was hard to find the heart in the medical system. Where is the heart when we are on hold while we listen to a recorded voice giving us the options of numbers to push for service? Where is the heart in the banking system when we make an honest mistake on a checking account and they add on charges because of it? There are so many examples. Everywhere I look, I see how we are being pulled into mind instead of heart. Meanwhile, there is this wonderful God calling us deeper into Him. We do not listen.

How do we give the heart, which we have been conditioned to ignore, its fair shake? How do we give God the space He needs to work inside us to heal us when we hardly know He's there? We don't. And we wonder why the world feels as though it is coming to the grips of chaos!

My relationship with God was growing stronger. I knew this by the way I felt looking forward to our conversations and by the way I began to hear His voice instead of the voice of criticism that I used to hear. Inside our heads, we all have the voice of a critical parent or teacher judging us. That voice is the voice of our egos; it neither inspires us nor gives us joy. The voice of God gave me joy, warmth, and a new, burning love that I never had experienced. I spoke with Him about this love, as I could talk with Him freely about anything. I knew He knew my heart, and there was no use even attempting to hide my feelings from Him.

"God, why is it so easy to love you? I feel as though I have found the long-lost love that I have hidden from others all my life, in You."

"Frannie, dear Frannie, you have always loved Me. How could you not love the One who gave you your heart? We have always been one together. How do you know love, except to have been given it first by Me? How do you know to wish for love, except once to have known what you yearn for now?"

"You are telling me that my love for You has always been there. Why, then, has it been so hidden from me?"

"You have walked away from what you wish for and toward the things you want."

"Explain, dear God. Explain."

"Wishes are dreams created by our union together. They are your heart's desire and will always bring you life. These are needs of your soul, and they are inside you. Wants are things your mind contrives only to be obtained outside of you. They deter you from your heart's wish: your search to find Me. They have you searching outside for what you only will find inside: Me."

The more space I gave to this relationship, the deeper it grew. My own mind's will was becoming less important. I found myself listening—in the mornings and periodically throughout the day—in the empty spaces I created. Often, in between students, I walked through the church gardens and sat on the bench where God and I would converse together. Soon I learned to hear God even with my students present, and I often asked Him how to respond to their questions. My own will was becoming thinner, and I listened to His will and His word instead.

The love between us grew and grew. This God, whom I never had heard before, had become the highlight of my life. This God was the missing piece of me. I felt filled and complete as I listened more and more, learning what He wished me to know. My relationship with my husband grew amazingly deeper, and I became more tolerant and compassionate. I no longer expected others to complete me. I was already whole. What I received from others became a gift. My husband and my family became priceless gifts in my life. It was as though the souls around me became the icing on a wondrous cake. My life felt filled with infinite gifts.

There was meaning everywhere I looked. God was in everything around me, inside me, and greater than what was around me and inside me. God was all and more. When I was with God, life was a blessing. Miraculous things happened. I could do things my mind told me were impossible. I was braver than I had ever been in my life as the beauty of life unfolded before my very eyes. I felt like a blossom, slowly opening its soft, wondrous petals to the warm and cozy light of the sun.

On a wondrous walk through the infinite shades of green, God spoke to me. I felt pulled by the nuns, even to the Catholic clergy, and I asked Him about this. I was developing a depth of compassion for those whose job it was to serve God and preach God but who were finding it difficult to feel God.

"Why me, God? Why, all of a sudden, does this Jewish girl wish to be a granter of wishes and dreams to the nuns and the Catholic clergy? This seems so out of character for me that it has to be Your will. Is it Your will, God?"

"You asked Me years ago how you, a tiny and fragile woman, could create peace in the world. You asked Me to lead the way. And now, when you have proven to Me that you could create the space to do this, and you have made My wish your life, I will give you a way to fulfill this wish.

"Some of My nuns are aging and becoming frail. Always serving me, their missions have taken some of the space they need for their inner journeys. Many priests are lost in old conditioning and thick structure. It is hard for them to find Me. They speak to Me but do not know Me. They connect with Me in ways that they have been taught, but their souls are in need of Me. They do not *feel* Me. They do not know Me, and yet they have a knowing that I Am. Their faith is what keeps them doing what they think they must do, as they have always done, yet their feelings are covered and more difficult to find beneath the shell that surrounds each of them. They live with their minds covering their hearts, and life feels heavy. They do not feel the depth of love I give them.

"You are to crack the shells to where I am, deep inside them. You are to bring them to Me so, once again, they can burn warmly with My love, helping to create peace in the world. This will be achieved as they hear My voice. And you are to teach them how to do this. This is part of our wish for peace. This is all I will tell you at present. Do not fill up any space with why or how or if it will happen. Fill it only with 'It will happen.'

"I am pulling the nuns. And with My word, one day the priests, too, will feel pulled. Slowly their faith will become less covered by structure and will be the breath of essence as which it began—a circle. War based upon dogma will end. Humanity shall see the need to be peace. If the Church is infused with My essence, the world will flow with peace. We shall begin with the Catholic Church, as its structure is heavy, and eyes fall upon it. Once its clergy hears My voice, I will give them instructions for My way to peace.

"Always speak as love to those who cross or parallel your path, as being love is the magic carpet on this journey. This work is only possible from one's heart. Wait to speak of this until one is coming from heart. My work cannot be done from one's mind. From the mind, it never looks possible.

"The people who will help you do not each have the same wish as you do, dear Frannie. They each will have their own wishes, and when put together, their wishes will become your wish. Each human being's wishes are the building blocks to make this greater wish reveal itself. Touch all you can. Each soul connecting with you will listen to your message—our message. Beware of those who try to control their destiny from mind. They are not ready. One must let go and allow for My will. Always honor My will, dear Frannie, over any of your thoughts. Obstacles may appear from mind. Be comforted that from heart there are never obstacles, only infinite ways and opportunities to create your wish. Go with the flow of My Word and the breadcrumbs that fall before you. Be love, be goodness, and be peace."

I asked God when this would happen. He shared with me that people were moving toward me and that even when I saw no action, there would be action. I was to rely only upon my faith in Him. And very slowly, the creed He gave me began to unfold in miraculous ways.

CHAPTER 14

When Prophecy Becomes Reality

The closer I felt to God, the more miraculous life became. Months passed after the creed was given to me, and an emergence of great, passionate energy stirred my work and my life. The world opened up into color as I observed even the smallest parts of nature. Things previously obscure became so beautiful. Great feelings of love infused me with unconditional acceptance of people and events—whether good or bad according to the mind's eye. Everything seemed doable, because it was not I who was doing it. It was God with me, or "We." I was keenly aware that everything, everywhere, was in God's court.

My husband was invited to a mid-winter hospital dinner for employees, and I remember being cold in my little black dress. I was tired and wished to be somewhere else. My attitude was so different that night than my usual feelings of grace and heaven. I sat up against a wall and was talking to my husband. He looked distracted to me, and I asked him what he saw. He squinted, trying to put into focus what caught his attention, and he told me he thought he saw the bishop standing in line by the bar.

Without thought, my cold and weary body bolted out of the chair, and before I knew it, I was making my way through the line at the bar. The legs that were carrying me felt as though they were on fire and no longer mine. My mind had no idea why I was walking over to the bishop, nor what I was going to say. I had never met a bishop before. There was no plan. There was no rehearsal, as one might have before talking with a man of such stature. I quickly walked up to him and asked a question that could not have come from me: "Bishop, I was wondering if I might come to speak with you sometime. Is that possible?"

The bishop's eyes were calm, and they sparkled with light—a light I had come to know on my journey as a breadcrumb from God. He spoke quietly, but with curiosity, and accepted my offer to come speak with him. He had no idea why I was standing there, and neither did I, but at that moment, a connection was made. The electricity stayed with me the rest of the evening as my mind tried to understand how I was led up to him and to ascertain what to discuss with him. There was no answer, and I drew a blank, thinking of this as a most interesting and impulsive event.

I let several months pass before contacting the bishop. There was confusion about e-mail addresses, and my mind could not fathom what I would say. Through my continued journaling with God, I was encouraged to keep the connection and e-mail the bishop. I was told that what I was to say would be there at the moment I needed it. Knowing that great faith would be necessary to pull off something with no plan and no knowing, I was glad when the time he selected was soon enough not to allow my mind to get in the way. I followed my heart and went to the bishop, ignorant of God's greater plan.

The bishop lived in a house only a block away from mine, down the street from the church where I taught, in a town that covers many square miles. It was a house I had passed many times before, with a large flagpole at the base of the driveway. I had looked at that house from a distance in the past, and I realized that I had been drawn to it for many years without knowing it belonged to a bishop or even what a bishop was.

I pulled into the circular driveway, put my car in park, and sat for a moment looking at the deep thunderhead clouds in the northwestern sky. I wondered what I was doing there and whether I should stay or run. As I opened the door of my car, a wind from the north rattled my white pants and blouse like a paper kite high in the skies. It blew me to the door, and once the kind man opened the door, a strong, surprise gust of wind blew me right into his house!

That wind was my cue that this meeting was not in my control. This meeting was God's meeting. Facing the bishop as we sat in comfortable living room chairs, his sparkling eyes looked with wonder as each word left my lips.

"So tell me, Frannie, why have you come to meet with me on this stormy day?" he asked.

I sat before him, thinking I was speechless, yet words were coming out of my mouth. The words were not mine. I would never have been caught dead in a bishop's house speaking with him from an empty mind!

I told him the story of what had happened to me—the same story I have told in these chapters. So much at home with what I was saying, I felt great peace within my heart. I told him about what I had been doing in teaching others to hear God's voice. Then, very surprisingly and most incredibly, I asked if he had ever heard God's voice.

He paused for a while and then spoke of the many ways God can be heard, but he quite clearly avoided a direct answer to the question.

I blurted, "May I teach you how to hear God's voice?"

He paused and looked down at his feet, sharing with me his need to discern my invitation.

Remembering forever his beautiful sparkle gaining intensity as he wondered about why I was there, I left quickly, giving him only my contact information. There was no pushing or prodding, as I was used to doing to make a point in my life. It was a simple question—an invitation to go deeper into the journey with God—an invitation to a God experience. We ended our meeting cordially, and I walked back to the car. The day had become as calm as a day can be. Not one clue remained that, earlier in the afternoon, the winds had been so strong as to push me into the bishop's life.

Months went by, and I did not hear from the bishop. I asked God why he did not respond, and God replied, "What you are impatient for will happen slowly, Frannie Rose."

One fine day, an e-mail fell out of the sky, inviting me back to the bishop's home to talk again about my invitation. Again, some time lapsed before I heard from him. Through this wondrous experience, God taught me about patience and how my mind could grab hold of this and create a story about God's intention. By the time I received the third e-mail from the bishop, my heart was at rest, and I knew to let go and let God do what God does best.

I met again with the bishop, and shortly after our work together began, he heard God's voice. Miraculously, he then sent priests to me, and they, too, are now hearing God. What we have found together—all of us—is that everything I experienced from the day I stood on the bridge forward—all that God has said to me, has come true.

We have looked at the scriptures together—something I never had read before, and we have read of Jesus's description of the Kingdom of Heaven. All He described, taught, and shared with those who listened were experienced by this Jewish girl who knew nothing about Him. What He was trying to say, in a most beautiful way, was that anyone, regardless of faith or religion, can take this journey. Anyone can have a relationship with God and feel His presence. God does not discriminate and loves us all equally. How would a Jewish girl, who had never learned of Jesus, hear what He was teaching from God? I continue to meet weekly with the bishop, and the lessons that unfold for both of us continue to this day.

CHAPTER 15

The Beginning of a New Vision of Peace

Many years have passed in my life since this story began. The walks through the greenery continue. Each day, I awaken to the present moment, grab my coffee and a journal, and sit quietly by the back door, awaiting sunrise. I observe paintings of beautiful pictures as God creates, with the colors of a rainbow, the skies of wonder and peace. I do not wish to miss these morning pictures.

One recent day, I sat by the back door, waiting for a touch of light on the dawn to see the spring colors brighten before my very eyes. Out of the door, I saw God giving birth to light as the leaves on trees were finally unwrinkled from the small branches out of which they squeezed. I saw the beauty of the purple lilacs against the orange of a newborn sky. This was a day like no other—a picture only seen doctored on a computer screen. I was awake to see it blossom before me into vivid color combinations I had never even imagined.

I had a conversation with God that I recorded in my journal—one most reflective of the journey so far. God asked me to walk with Him because He wished to show me something down by the lake. I quickly ate my breakfast and started down toward the beauty of the lake with a stirring excitement in my heart.

It felt as though I would never get there that day—as if my feet were too small for the large steps I wished to take. I remembered years ago God's words to me as my mind urged me to run: *What you are impatient for will happen slowly.*

I slowed down when I heard those words and glanced around me at the beauty that was surrounding my body walking quickly to the lake. The new color of spring coated the trees with what looked like velvet, and I stopped to stare at the sharp point of treetops against a deep blue sky.

"God, there are so many gifts surrounding me. Are You here with me now?"

All at once, the blue heron, my symbol of peace and freedom, flew above my head and landed softly on my side of the lake.

"Frannie Rose, a gift for you. We are to talk about the peace of the blue heron. We are to speak about creating peace in the world."

"I have worked to show You that I have heard Your call to me, dear God. I know that You exist. What's more, I have seen the miracles You have created in my life and in the lives of my students. Where do You wish me to go from here?" I asked.

"Sweet Frannie Rose, look over at the blue heron. Does he not live a life of peace? When he stands next to other birds, he does so with harmony, with grace, and with love. He allows them their space. He hears me, Frannie Rose. And he is always free to fly above the noise and strife when the other birds cannot find a peaceful solution to their differences."

"Fly above, yes, I have seen this. I have seen him leave and fly above dissension and things that interfere with his solitude. And I understand that he can do this, but I do not have wings, dear God, so how might I react?"

"You, too, can fly above the animosity and turmoil of the world. I have given you inner wings. You have found them. Use them and fly."

"You have given me a sense of freedom, dear God. Is this what you refer to as inner wings? For surely, anatomically we are not able to fly in the sky."

"Use your inner wings, Frannie Rose, and teach others to do the same. Fly while finding peace within your heart. I am your wings, dear Frannie Rose. Share this peace with those you see in passing. It is transmitted not by your words but through your being. Simply be peace."

I looked over at the blue heron, and everything he did emitted peace. There was a solace in his standing there, a haven for those who are weary. I was able to watch him and be with him and feel his peace-filled heart.

"Frannie Rose," God said, "I wish you to tell your students something that is very important about peace in the world. I wish you to tell them to speak to Me about their part in creating peace. Each human being has a special part in this, a building block that I wish to give each one. Let them come to Me for the answer so that they, too, may hear Me and become peace in your world.

"Remember, Frannie Rose, religion is just a vehicle. It is not the answer. I am the answer. I am. I am in the center of all. Religion was created to bring human beings to Me. There is truth within all religion. Find it in the center. Let religion become for man rich history and beauty beyond where your minds can take you. And beyond religion, there is Me. Tell your students to let their religion take them to My world—to peace and not away from it."

I felt God's words deeply as I stood there overlooking the lake that day, with the blue heron next to me on the shoreline. I looked out onto the stillness of snow-covered mountain peaks against the blueness of the sky. What a wondrous way to live my life. What beauty and peace my heart felt.

Every religion is a piece of the pie of faith, and all pieces meet in the center: God. This center is the place from which we work and pray. And when we are there together, we are at peace, we are harmony, and we are what He asks us to be—different breeds and colors of flowers in a beauty-filled garden of Him.

The girl who spent seventeen years of her life becoming empty had been given new life. She became able to do everyday activities with a sense of aliveness and peace. Though her disease is treatable, it is not cured. Even so, inside her heart, she knows she will never be bound to it again. Her life is free with God and the greenery now. Through a simple act of surrender, she has been healed. Always and in all ways her heart bursts with gratitude. She feels the peace of God flowing through her veins. God has created within her heart a miraculous transformation. The first, wondrous day this empty girl stood on a bridge overlooking a mountain lake, asking God if she could help Him create peace in the world, became the day this peace began—the peace she now can give to the world. This was the gift of many years of suffering without God. It all began in the heart of an empty girl standing on a bridge and, for the first time, listening deeply to the God within her heart.

There is much resistance and strife in our world. We focus on identifying differences rather than on finding our mutual center in

God. If we were to find this center, a message from God surely would change the world in miraculous ways.

The spiritual environment in the world is changing. People are moving deeper toward the interior journey, the journey that I took, to find an experience of God through hearing His voice. With constant conversation, this experience soon becomes a relationship that far surpasses anything a human mind could dream. It is a most sacred relationship between being and Creator. To be so fulfilled and so whole is a beautiful way to touch the world. All who begin this relationship, upon hearing God's voice, find that the beauty of the Infinite far surpasses anything their minds might think to create. Their lives are forever changed by knowing their Creator. They find a Kingdom within them. This Kingdom of Heaven—the greenery— lives within all of us. It lives within Him.

PART

II

The Teachings

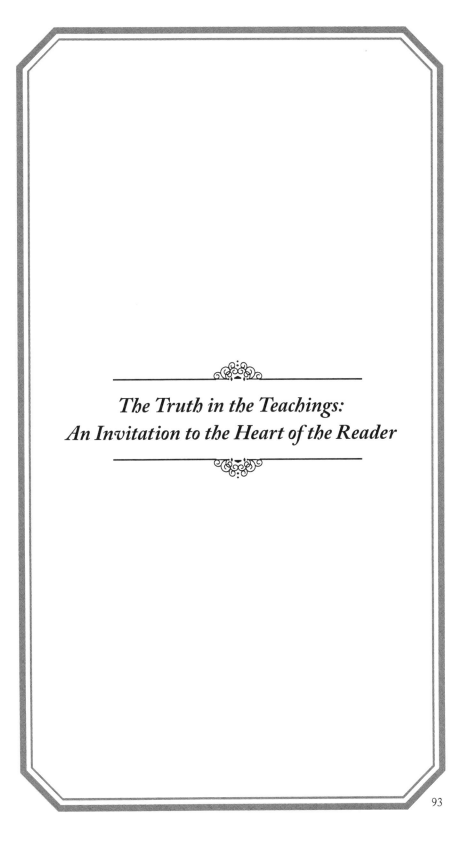

The Truth in the Teachings:
An Invitation to the Heart of the Reader

Accumulated over months and years, most of the teachings God has given me are held in seventy-five notebooks. These teachings have not come to me at consistent times or places. Many times, I have not been able to write down the teachings in the moment, as I have been outside without a means to record them.

Over the years, I have created retreats and workshops to give the world what God wished me to share. The timing of the teachings for these retreats has been unpredictable. God has given them to me when He felt it was time. Many times, a retreat has been scheduled for only a few days away, and I have asked God for the teaching. In this exercise, He has taught me patience and a keen awareness of focusing on the present moment—because that is the only space where He is.

When I became focused on the future, I discovered that I could not find God. I would speak, but my mind would interfere with my listening. I knew this was the filled-up space of which God had spoken, and upon not hearing His voice, I quickly learned to clear my inner space. Our awareness of God grows from within the emptiness and not the filled space inside of us.

I am sharing some of these teachings in this book, as God intended. I ask you to read them in presence, with only this moment in your heart. God cannot be found in the past; although that is where your mind sometimes wishes you to be, it is not where He is. God cannot be found in the future, although that is where your mind will try to keep you so that it stays in charge of your life.

I ask that you allow the message to go to your heart, which means not getting attached to the words. Words are merely containers that hold thoughts, and thoughts are limited by our limited minds. That which grows within your heart is infinite and cannot be contained, boxed, or captured precisely in a word, for most of it will fly freely away from you. The essence of life that is within your heart breaks away from any restrictions that are placed upon it, for it is naturally free, as seeds are, to travel through the winds.

Ultimately, you will have to answer this question: Do you wish to allow your mind to steer your life, or do you wish for God's will to guide you? This is a question that will take you through many leaps of faith. Do you trust your image of God enough to allow for His will in your life, or are you going to resist His will and decide what is best for your destiny? Are you going to go with the flow of life, or are you going to fight the flow of life?

Please read these teachings slowly, in the present moment at a time of space and reflection. It is best not to read more than one each day, as you will need patience, awareness, flexibility, and surrender to create the openness for God to ripen the fruits of these teachings in your life.

CHAPTER 16

The Seeking

"What you are searching for is your deepest longing.
What is inside of this longing?
I am."

Everyone is searching. Everywhere you go, you run into seekers who are out and about, searching for something. Whether we speak—in the spiritual sense—literally or figuratively, this is what most people do all day long. Some have jobs that require searching for answers, searching for questions, searching for future answers, or searching for future solutions. Some have jobs that require searching the past to see what has or has not worked before. Some search for knowledge by attending schools. Others search for new ways do things—new techniques, new combinations, new drugs, new diseases, and new ideas. Some people spend their weekends searching for the right antiques, the most beautiful homes, or the fanciest cars. Some go out on weekend shopping sprees, searching for something to fill their emptiness—the right clothes, the right fragrance, the right shoes, or the right underwear. Most of us spend our entire lives searching. Any satisfaction we experience is short-lived, and soon, we begin a search for something new. Some people never experience life beyond the searching. What are *you* searching for?

What we do outside of us is merely a reflection of what is happening within us, for all behaviors begin from a deeper place inside. The need to search speaks to a deeper longing. Longing for what? What kind of longing will never be satisfied by searching outside one's Self? The answer is so simple: a longing whose solution is found inside one's Self.

Take a moment to search through your thoughts. You may be trying to search to find something wrong with this idea. Please search away! Our minds have taken us on a ride our whole lives. They have imprisoned our hearts and decided to take us on a fruitless search. With small amounts of temporary satisfaction, we continue to allow them to lead us on to the next search, a bigger search, a more distracting search, and a search with more fruitful rewards. Then, one day, we finally sit down with all the things we could ever want around us, and we realize that we are tired of searching and still feeling empty inside. We wonder what our lives really have come to as we stare at the items we own all around us, and our hearts weep with the knowing that our deepest hunger has not been satisfied.

What is our deepest hunger? It begins with connection to the deepest part of us, our true Self. We wish to know that we are not alone. When our minds are weary from thinking all day long, our deepest hunger wishes to turn off our thoughts and be with our hearts. And the deepest part of our hearts is God; this is where we connect with our Creator.

Take a moment to look at yourself. How long does the satisfaction of "finding" appease you? How long before a new car becomes an old car and you begin to search again? Do you ever experience complete satisfaction from your searching? You don't! This does not happen. As human beings, we unknowingly *live to search*. We live to search for a reason to live.

An object or a doing on the outside of yourself can never satisfy your every need, but realizing the wholeness inside of you *can* satisfy your every need. "What wholeness?" you ask. Ah, but this is only the beginning of the journey inside to find out.

CHAPTER 17

Your True Self

"You are not who you think you are."

Deep within your Self, you contain the miracles of God's creations since the beginning of time. You contain elements of the sun and small particles of the big bang. You contain the genetic makeup of those who came before you, and what you are and what you make of your Self becomes part of the legacy you leave for those who come after you.

One question we all ask at some time in our lives far surpasses the importance of any other question we ask of life or of God: who am I? It's a question loved by philosophers and psychologists. It's a question that has been asked for centuries by those unknowing of the answer.

We are a spark of God-Self. God is the life within us and the very essence of our spirit. We each were created as a union between man and God, and at one time, this union was the only thing we knew. God nurtured the seeds within our hearts and helped us to grow in compassion, kindness, goodness, love, freedom, hope, generosity, and gratitude. Each of us has experienced life in ways that help grow these seeds, and the unique manifestation of their growth is who we are.

How do we know love with another? We know this love because of the love we have been given since life began from God. How do we know when love is lacking in a relationship? We know because of the perfect love we always have had from God. Our union with God completes us in every way when we look inward. When we look outward for completion, we find we never can be satisfied entirely. First, we must have a consciousness of God's love.

If God completes us, then what are we to one another? Why do we try to find total satisfaction with another human being if it is God to whom we should be looking? We mistakenly look outside ourselves before we look inside to be completed. If we were to turn to God first, we would find that every human being who comes toward us with love is simply God's gift to us—icing on the cake of perfection.

What we have done since society conditioned our minds is walk away from this union with God. As in the parable of the prodigal son,[1] we have walked away from God and all we can be given by

---

[1]   A parable of Jesus, recounted in Luke 15:11–32.

turning inward. Instead, we attempt to find it outside ourselves. By looking outside ourselves for the answers instead of inside, we find ourselves on an endless search leading nowhere. When we finally realize this, we walk back toward the union with God and find happiness through the only way we ever were meant to be complete.

If we were to stop trying to make who we are dependent upon what we are, we would be happy. It is in the looking always for something more that we never can find solace. There is no end to more and no end to trying to create more. If you leave it up to your mind and not your heart, your mind will always look for more. This is the perfect recipe for unhappiness. You must remember who you are as your union with God: We.

If you saw a tulip, you could say that its flower has a certain shape, color, and vibrancy. Our true Self contains this vibrancy, or energy, that is our special pattern of life itself. This pattern—this intensity, passion, and flow—is ours to share with God. It is part of who we are.

Who you are is not about what you do, and it is not about how others treat you or what you have done with your life. Who you are is your birthright—simply, your union with God—We. Each person manifests awareness of this with unique intensity, passion, and flow. You are each, in your own unique ways, a union of the seen and the unseen. If you live this consciously, life will hold a deeper meaning and will bring you great joy and peace.

CHAPTER 18

———⁓•◦◦⊙◦◦•⁓———

The Prison of Mind

"Those walls and locked doors are only within your mind.
You have within you
the keys to the Kingdom."

God had asked me to do a workshop on heart, mind, and destiny, and as I awaited the teaching, time was running short. I had only several days left to prepare, and it was a leap of faith to take sign-up forms from attendees when I was unsure how the workshop was to be.

Two days before the workshop, I saw from my bed an eastern star shining brightly in my bedroom window. It was 4:00 a.m., and I quickly got out of bed and grabbed a fleece robe. I put on the coffee and picked up my journal and pencil to write. Before I was completely awake, my pencil moved swiftly on paper, and a diagram slowly came to me.

The diagram looked very complex when it was complete, and I felt skeptical that it was from God, as never before had He given me something so complex. I wondered how I would present such complexity to a group of people without confusing them and bringing them deep into thought. I knew I had to take a leap of faith and that I would know when the time was right. The day of the workshop, it became clear to me that the diagram was to be presented from the inside out.

Earlier in the book, I spoke of how God explained to me the spark of life within us that has been present since the day we, as life, began. This spark of life is the God center, and it is at the very core of our being.

The God Center

Presence
I AM = TRUTH (LIFE)

It is life, acceptance of the present moment, and the observer of what is now, which can be represented in the words "I am."

As a baby emerges from the birth canal, he or she awakens to the present moment. The baby's brain monitors the outside world from a place of acceptance, and from this God center, a heart center grows around it. Within that center of one's being is emergence of the true Self.

God + The Seeds of the Spirit = True Self
"WE"

Sees with the eyes of a child

Within this true Self, much like within the core of an apple, are the spiritual seeds that God has given us. This is a world of beauty and a world of love. The seeds of goodness, faith, generosity, gratitude, joy, hope, love, and peace are among the seeds that God planted. With the awakening of this part of an infant, eyes are alert to what is in the environment around him. He sees from an empty place as he is not old enough to know to fill it. The eyes of a child begin here. These are the eyes of wonder and the eyes of awe.

When a baby's thinking mind matures and begins to see that every action causes a reaction, the baby learns to manipulate his environment. From experience, he learns that employing his mind works; a cry may get him cuddling, and sometimes a wet diaper will result in a clean diaper and nurturing. A baby learns quickly that cooing creates a smile from a parent and that continuing to coo results in more smiling. The reinforcement for using their minds is that babies can obtain what they want from outside their *Selves*. Because the satisfaction from obtaining what they want is transient, babies learn to continue using their minds to perpetuate self-gratification. The mind learns that it is better to be turned on than off. This process is only the beginning of a mind that self-perpetuates.

The sense of wonder and innocence leaves us as we grow into young children and are taught by others to fill the emptiness with thinking and conditioning. As a child begins to grow and reaches the toddler years, he learns that some things are considered right and some are considered wrong. The trial-and-error processes of learning are sometimes met with stern looks or firm "no" answers. In some cases, children are not met with patience and are spanked and hurt as a consequence. Regardless of the nature of the negative response by the mom or dad, a child learns quickly that compliance elicits a positive response, thereby establishing an action-reaction connection engraved in the mind. These engravings revolve around a child's mind in circles, creating action similar to that of a merry-go-round. Thoughts go into this merry-go-round, and they never come out. They stay there and become trapped there, unable to escape. This merry-go-round is the "mind prison."

The Mind Prison
The True Self is covered and trapped by conditioning.

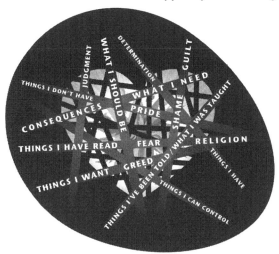

This is where we get caught.

From the time of early childhood all the way through one's life, the mind fills. It fills with knowledge, and it fills with consequences. It fills with wants from the outside and ways to obtain them. At first, the mind is used to acquire things from the outside in order to live—food, warmth, clothing, and comfort. However, over time, a filled mind—what I call a mind prison—develops with a stronger will and an appetite for more than simply food or sustenance. It wants more things added to itself constantly, and it fills up with thought obsessively.

Outside the mind prison, the mind creates a shell to protect itself. This shell, the "ego shell," is similar to that of an egg, although many, many layers of shell form around the mind prison. Each consequence for our actions creates another layer of shell, encasing the mind prison and keeping one's focus around it. As the mind fills more and more, it revolves and becomes increasingly heavier. It craves more, and with more, it requires more shell to protect itself.

The Ego Shell
Layers of untruth
Our perceptions and stories

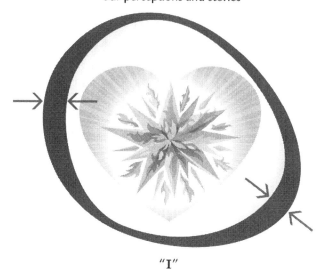

"I"

The outside world bombards this shell constantly. The shell begins to develop a response to that. When something from the mind is questioned or insulted, the shell gets thicker to self-protect. Each time the shell is bombarded, it grows thicker again to self-protect, fearing loss. Within a period of time in a child's life, the ego is created, and a child learns that her sense of worth in the world depends upon how the world reacts to her mind. This is living in a world of perception. In other words, she becomes her ego.

What happens to the spiritual center we call the true Self? It is pushed down beneath a heavy mind. The mind becomes so greedy that it wants more and more to hold. The more it has to hold, the more mind stuff revolves around it, giving us more about which to think. This illustrates the human condition that Eckhart Tolle describes as being "lost in thought."[2] The Self is lost, weighed down by a heavy mind busily chewing on mind candy. At such times, we say things like "My heart is heavy," or "I feel so burdened."

---

[2]   Eckhart Tolle, *The Power of Now* (Novato: New World Publishing, 2004).

What is unknown to us most of our lives is that, within each of us, the heart—though imprisoned beneath this heaviness—cries to us to set it free. We hear it from time to time in the form of longings. We feel longings for love, hope, joy, and compassion. We feel it in our wishes and dreams. Often, we push these feelings aside, catering to the mind prison that constantly demands our immediate attention. Sometimes we do this consciously, and other times, we do it unconsciously because our minds have total hold on us. So begins a life of continuous conflict between the mind prison and the heart. Inside the center of this heart, pressed down by all this mind stuff and covered, is God.

Our lives are in a constant state of mind/heart conflict. The conflict manifests through the decisions we make when we feel "torn" or through feelings of suffering. The struggle we feel is the mind going around in the mind prison regarding a decision that needs to be made from a different place, the heart. The mind prison revolves and becomes heavy with a decision that is most difficult for it to make, often one it is unable to resolve. It is only when we walk away from the thoughts of this situation, and move into our hearts, that the freedom to feel our way through the decision is found. Almost always, it is a heart answer and not a solution our minds could have produced.

To see this takes space—space away from the endless revolutions of the mind—and time to listen to the heart. Time is a commodity that we fill up with things to do. Our minds keep us very busy with task after task. There is no time or space to reflect. Time or space to feel is considered a luxury by our minds. It is viewed as the least important priority. Could we imagine telling the boss at work that we need an afternoon to feel?

In truth, our society values a busy life far more than it does a life of space. Most of us are in a whirlwind. Our lives are moving endlessly, without stopping. Awakening in the morning begins a series of movements, from here to there and from there to somewhere else. The sound of the alarm signals the jump out of bed—out of stillness, quiet, and peace—and into a world defined by action.

Our lives are no different than the metaphor of rats in a maze. What a distaste we have for this metaphor! And yet, where are the differences? The rat wanders aimlessly around the maze to find the cheese it wants to eat. Do we not do the same thing, day in and day out in the mind prison, filling up space either making the money to buy "things" or buying the things themselves?

What is the answer? Space to *be*. We need to take space in between things we do to listen to our hearts. When we cannot solve something, we need to step away from it, knowing it must be given to the heart. Perhaps we need the space in which to see the answer. When we give the heart that space to grow, the answers will come. It may take a while, but if we create the space in which to see it, it will be.

What happens when adversity hits our lives? It hits the shell that we call the ego, and if the hit is hard enough and deep enough, it will crack the shell and open it from the center outward, much like cracking the shell of an egg. The cracking of the ego shell can occur in small amounts throughout a lifetime, with insults to the ego and small adverse life situations, or all at once in a difficult lifetime adversity. One can lose her job and lose her identity, thereby cracking the shell to the center.

One day the searching feels empty.
We face adversity or immense discomfort.

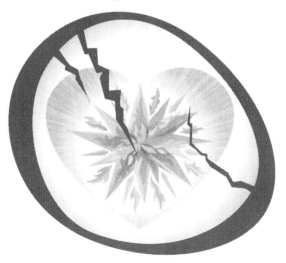

With enough resistance, the shell of Ego cracks.

Another person might experience a life-threatening illness and reprioritize his life, deeming the things he holds dear no longer important. Losing one's identity through difficult life situations cracks the ego shell. When this happens, God escapes through the cracks and blankets us with His peace.

When the Ego Shell breaks...

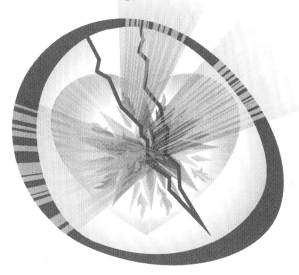

...GOD escapes through the cracks.

Adversity can be a life-changing event, leading one toward faith and longing for God, or something soon forgotten while a new layer of ego shell grows, covering the true Self again.

CHAPTER 19

—⁓•⌒⊙⌒•⁓—

On Our State of Being

"Human beings need more space in their lives—space to be, space to feel their freedom, and space to reflect upon their lives, feeling inside their hearts what they wish for."

Most of us feel the world is asking a lot of us. There are so many demands from others on our time and space. We do many things to please others and thereby gratify our egos, but what do we do for our hearts? When was the last time you remember watching a sunset when nothing else was going on? Without thought? Without worry? Without thinking about the things you wanted to do and needed to do? Without thinking of things you wanted to buy or money you had to make? Have you spent time without thinking lately? When was the last time you "listened" to silence?

Our lives have become busier and busier. Our typical priorities are getting things accomplished and creating things that show what we produced for our time spent. Often, we feel a need to hold something in our hands in order to say that we have not *wasted time*—that our time actually was spent on something concrete. What is "wasting time"? To each of us, it means something different, depending upon the values our parents taught us. Our world evaluates us based upon how much we produce, how much cash flow we create, and how busy we are. How did this all come about?

As human beings became more and more intellectual, acquiring education in specific fields and assessing self-worth based on our incomes and how much knowledge we could obtain, our mind prisons worked overtime. We began living with the illusion that the secrets of life could be found outside of the true Self and grabbed from the outside world. We decided to take the things we want and let go of the things for which we wish.

What did you do, and what did you value yesterday? You might remember the doings and the new things bought, but do you remember the inverse, your "downtime" when you did absolutely nothing at all? How about the time you spent looking within your own heart, being introspective?

Our mind prisons are so heavy and turn so fast that we have lost sight of our hearts' desires—our true Self. Throughout the history of humankind, with great minds have come great egos, the thick shells that cover our hearts and souls. The human ego has grown larger with each generation until we have traveled so far from our hearts and have become so busy in our minds that we no longer have the ability to touch inside of us; we miss entirely the place where we connect deeply with God, or our Creator. If we feel this place and live in it, life is pure joy. This is the Kingdom of Heaven of which Jesus spoke. Is that where you live?

CHAPTER 20

On Our Conditioning

"See My world not with your eyes, but with My eyes.
Look at My world with the eyes of a child."

When I was sick in my bed, it never occurred to me that I was not living from my heart. In fact, during that time of adversity, I was farther from my heart than ever before. I knew I had feelings, and I wished to be well, but I did not know that what kept me sick was all the fighting my mind was doing with my heart. The heart simply wishes to be free, but the mind keeps it trapped beneath the mind prison. There were no solutions in the mind prison, but I saw this as a reason to stay there. I was unaware of the infinite possibilities that were available in my heart. To my mind, surrender meant "giving up." I believed the old saying I heard in my childhood years, "God helps those who help themselves."

To many people, one's own will, or the mind's will, is of utmost importance. We pray in church and in temple about God's will, but we do not stop to consider the difference. To live by the mind's will is not living from the heart. To live by the heart is living by God's will, for the heart and God's will are one.

We are born as close to God as we can be—a living essence—a bundle of love. We are born to parents who may nurture us and love us and likely use their minds to teach us right from wrong and good from bad.

Society tells us how to behave and how we must conform to the rules that have been made for us in order to live together in peace. Many of us have lived long enough to know that these rules are made to create order in the home and in the school environment. Over time, as the rules increase in complexity and depth, the living bundle of love becomes an egg yolk covered in shell. The essence of who we are becomes lost underneath the structure and rules of society. We comply by continuing to follow the rules for the sake of rule-following, thereby losing the instinct to follow our hearts.

As a child gets older, school begins, and school brings more rules about "how to be" and how to perform. The mind of a child becomes conditioned in an eight-hour day of constant bombardment by thought. The child's heart is pushed deep underneath, no longer appearing in the school. Feelings are seldom spoken of, and thought becomes pervasive. We are taught that we need to have strong minds because the heart is weak. We are taught to trust our minds and not our hearts. By being conditioned in this way, more thickness is continually added to the shell, keeping the heart depressed and bound.

Our schools value thought, mind, and ego. Productivity is sacred. Space and time are managed carefully as students are paraded from one class to another. Little time is spent in between classes to socialize, because keeping children out of trouble and on task is valued most. When the day is finally over and the mind is tired, there is homework to do, or there are physical activities to pursue. Every free moment of space in time is filled. All the empty space is infused with activity.

In high school, future thinking is at its peak. High school becomes a means to an end—to get into a good college. Students study for good grades, apply to colleges, and wait to hear about their futures. They anticipate the answers. The present moment no longer exists for either parent or child. The future is all that matters. Rules and structure have given way to future thinking, and there is no longer a present moment in which to live.

From there, careers take flight, and thinking about the future becomes a way of living. Each career step is based upon the mind's anticipation of where a given path might lead. A present moment, again, is reduced to a means to an end—in this case, a greater career path.

And what of the heart? It lies beneath the many layers of shell that cover it, bound and dormant. As the emptiness from future thinking begins to give way to loneliness and feelings of being lost, the heart tries hard to speak. *I have everything I have ever wanted, but I feel this emptiness inside me. Why do I not feel any sense of gratification from having what I have worked toward my whole life?*

If one takes more than a few moments to sit with that question, and really tries to feel the answer, the heart will awaken. However, most do not attempt to wait for its call. From within the emptiness, God within your heart calls and wishes to give you the answer. The mind gets in the way, trying to fill the space with things and more things or thoughts to appease it. But the space cannot be filled with things; instead, the heart must sit still in the space, allowing the seeds planted within it long ago to break free.

It is from within the emptiness and space in one's life that the seeds within can begin to take root and grow. They require light to shine on them, water to nourish them, and space in which to grow. In a crowded garden, with little time to tend the flowers, weeds soon take over. In an empty garden, with sprouting seeds, light, water, and a conscientious caretaker, a beautiful garden can grow. From the emptiness, the heart can break through the shell of mind, ego, and thought. The heart expands, growing as fragrant blossoms in colors that only the imagination held before. From within the heart, a garden grows. It is filled with hopes, long-ago dreams, and desires—flowers that stir the heart and fill the garden with fresh blossoms never unveiled in any other season.

How do we know our hearts' desires? We let go of thinking about them, and we begin to feel about them. We create space in our lives for feelings, quiet, and our journey within. We learn to feel the present moment and live in it, letting go of future and outcomes, as they invariably are affected by the element of grace. We observe the thinker. We realize that truth changes with every season and in every moment in time, and it is subject to the eyes that perceive it. We allow space for love, hope, faith, and God, for they are as much a part of the garden as the infinite colors of the blossoms.

Thought and mind are the biggest obstacles between God and us. Deep within our hearts lies our connection to God. If one is in a place of mind, one cannot be in a place of heart. The mind is a tool to be employed, but the heart is the beacon that takes us to God. The mind leads us by thinking, but the heart leads us by feeling. We learn to feel the things that speak to us, and we learn to feel the present moment, living in presence as much as we can.

Since childhood, we have been conditioned to listen to our minds and not to our hearts. The results we have achieved are by way of thoughts—our thoughts and other people's thoughts. However, thoughts can be wrong. Thoughts cannot fulfill our hearts. It is like putting a round peg into a square hole. Thoughts only fill our minds. They are empty—without depth, dimension, or infinite potential. Success feels one-dimensional without the element of heart. Our new journey begins with the inverse. It begins with the heart employing the mind.

Deciding to take the inner journey is the beginning of a path for which there are no words, only feelings. With each step taken forward, one finds wisdom, depth, and meaning passed over many times before. From a place of heart, one begins an adventure of infinite possibilities—an adventure of hope, love, joy, and God. It is a journey that forever changes an individual and the direction of his life from a mind-led journey to a journey by way of the heart.

CHAPTER 21

Your Life amidst Life Situations

"There is no need to suffer.
Suffering is your signal to call to Me.
I will diffuse your suffering.
Turn inward to Me."

The mind prison loves to be occupied and filled to its saturation point. In fact, the heavier it is, the more of a sense of ego we have. We establish a victim identity through being busy and having "too much to do." It makes the ego feel important and meaningful. The more the mind prison and the ego are needed, the more inflexible we become with our time, space, and thoughts.

With more of a heavy mind, the heart is bound by its heaviness. There is no room for it to find avenues of escape to provide a fresh outlook on a situation. Thoughts remain rigid, with no access to feelings. The body fatigues, and weariness sets in. When something unexpected falls from the sky, the mind feels discomfort and threat. It basks in its regimen, organization, and habit. In other words, it thrives on resisting change.

When something unknown to the mind prison and its highly maintained organization falls into our lives, the discomfort that this change creates throws our minds into a tailspin. They detest having to make adjustments to what they view as firm, leaving the life situation adverse. Often, we say, "This can't be," or "Why does this always happen to me?" In truth, both of these responses signify resisting what is already true, what already is. Change is part of growth and part of living. Resistance is futile—and fruitless!

As the mind prison becomes busier, it causes us to live in denial or resistance by creating stories that take us away from dealing directly with a situation. The mind calls these stories "problems," and with negativity attached to them, we no longer view them as simple circumstances. The negative energy these circumstances take on gives the mind a reason to continue revolving and weighing down the heart.

Can you see the difference between the gift of life itself and a life situation? The problems in our lives are really only situations to which negative thoughts have been applied. Our lives are beneath these situations, as the sky is to the clouds that cover it. When we have a problem, we forget the life that exists beneath it. We allow the problem to color our lives, much like the way we allow the clouds in the sky to limit a cloudy day by calling it "a nasty day."

There is life in the spiritual center of the heart. It is God. It is the awareness that you exist, or "I am." This is the most profound part of us, yet the *simplest* part of us. When we lose sight of this, and we become the life situation instead of a life, we lose a sense of God in our existence entirely.

Most of us speak from a place of mind or ego. In fact, when we use the word "I," it almost always refers to the part of us that is the ego. When we address problems, dealing with life situations without the sense that there is life behind them, we are living from ego.

Simply put, a problem is not one until the mind decides to create a story around the situation. Once a situation becomes a problem, the mind uses it as a magnet to pull us back to it whenever our alliance wavers and moves toward the heart. This is how the mind perpetuates, and this is how it dominates one's life. Drama and negativity are then attracted to us and to those with whom we come in contact. The life in the day becomes that problem. Life is no longer paved with awareness, patience, and surrender. Instead, it is paved with tension, stress and strife.

CHAPTER 22

On Negativity

"You cannot change another.
Be instead what you wish to see.
Let all negativity move you to be the change."

How negative are you? Do you often go to work feeling resistant to new ideas and new ways to do things you have done before? Do you have a coworker who complains, and do you always listen to that person's complaints? Do you find yourself drained instead of energized by a good day's work? If you answered yes to these questions, it might be a good idea to become aware of the negativity moving toward you.

Do you seek teamwork and peace in your workplace? Wishing to radiate peace and be God-centered, we must have an awareness of what we unconsciously absorb from outside us. When we are busy in "work mode," things often come at us quickly and without our realizing it … until we take a moment for reflection. Bombarded with negativity in many forms—news broadcasts, e-mail, newspapers, phone calls, and one another—we can be blind to how it touches us.

Negativity slowly erodes our sense of possibility, replacing it with a fear-based storyline. Our minds can rush into "protective mode," limiting what before was our sense of the Infinite. We begin to perceive the glass as half-empty rather than as half-full. The mind works quickly to access old pain reactions and related experiences, sending forth their feelings to fuel this energy's intensity. Even though past feelings are irrelevant to a current situation, they add power to the negative message, increasing our desire to share the story with someone else.

Someone who shares a negative story gets a sense of self from being the one to relay it to others, perpetuating the negative energy. Unknowingly, the one who shares this story sets into action a chain of events that can bring an office from a place of productivity to a day of standstill! Office negativity can brew much like a perfect storm, causing winds and fallout that greatly impede an organization's productivity.

According to Gary Topchik:

> Negativity is a virus that spreads rapidly from one person to another. Individuals may bring the virus to work or catch it from others in an organization. The negativity virus spreads quickly in a matter of

days or weeks, and once transmitted, it is difficult to cure. The effects of negativity are devastating to any organization and can lead to increased turnover, lateness, absenteeism, customer complaints, errors, accidents, and illness, all resulting in deep bottom-line costs.[3]

Added to these unfortunate effects in an organization, once the employee goes home, he or she spreads the negativity to family. Manifesting mildly as a negative mood, it may explode into an argument with a spouse or a child. A person caught up in negativity has no space inside himself for listening with objectivity. Negativity expands inside a person so that much of what he hears takes on a negative tone. There is even less room for openness or negotiation. When a negative response is, in turn, shared with a family member, that person's mind expands with this negativity, and off to work or school he goes.

If new ideas are being introduced in the workplace or school, one who harbors negativity can be resistant. The person's inner mind space is too filled with the negativity that has already expanded within. One becomes resistant to doing things a new way or making adaptations and changes in work or behavior.

Eckhart Tolle said, "All inner resistance is experienced as negativity in one form or another. All negativity is resistance. In this context, the two words are almost synonymous."[4]

Our job as human beings is to leave this world a better place for the greater good. Each one of us can help clear the air of negativity. How do we do this? By being aware of what is coming our way and not allowing it to penetrate. Instead of responding to negativity by sharing a negative story, we can take a moment to see the flipside.

---

[3]   Gary Topchik, *Managing Workplace Negativity* (New York: AMACOM, 2001).
[4]   Eckhart Tolle, *The Power of Now* (Novato: New World Publishing, 2004).

Is something being suggested as a way to solve a problem at work? Perhaps we have tried this technique before, but it didn't work. We can feel the present moment as a new moment—with its own sense of possibility. With acceptance, we can give it another try!

In the spirit of peace and becoming the change we wish to see in the world, each of us must first accept what already is. It is this acceptance that gives us the positive energy or flexibility for change through opening up to God. Embracing change and flexibility gives our businesses the chance to succeed. Negativity ensures failure.

Negativity is a psychic disease. It is contagious. Resistance stops all positive energy dead in its tracks, preventing flow or change. The way of life and the way of God is the way of change and flow. Negativity involves stepping away from God, for negativity is resistance to God's flow.

In your workspace, be peace and be present. Become aware of negativity for the sake of your own journey as well as for the benefit of your coworkers and the ones you love. None of us helps the world by spreading negativity, yet we surely can help the world by becoming aware of it. See the flipside of negativity by shining a light on the present moment through your awareness. Change the story, and share it in a way of hopefulness and possibility. You will be helping your Self, your family, and your workplace with your positive gift to the world.

CHAPTER 23

On Understanding Expectations

"Expect nothing.
And be free to see everything."

How much life do you really experience when your mind is set upon expectations and anticipating what will happen? Are you likely to get what you expect? How often do you miss the whole picture when you are looking for something you think you'll see? Does it detract from your enjoyment when something does not meet your expectations?

What is an expectation? The dictionary defines it as "a belief that something will happen or is likely to happen."[5] Let us focus then on the key concept of belief. We hold on tightly to our beliefs, but do they really help us? Beliefs are ideas that the ego uses to reinforce its sense of self. When we have expectations, the ego gets a sense of self by keeping us fixated on future events. This future is where the mind can be in control. This is where the mind reigns. The mind believes it will see what it expects, while the ego gets its sense of self from being right or wrong about the expectation. When the ego is right, we get a positive sense of self that we are right, and when the ego is wrong, we get a negative sense of self from not doing it right.

Both the concepts of belief and expectation strengthen the ego, whether the mind is right or wrong. The mind uses belief to judge or compare oneself with others, and it uses expectations to keep us anchored in the future, where it has the most control. In doing this, we cannot be in the present moment where we are free and can feel the presence of God. The mind has us always seeing with the eyes of the ego instead of seeing with the eyes of God.

Let us suppose that we are viewing a mountaintop, expecting to see a sugarcoated mountaintop. The "egoic mind" asks our eyes to glance to the top of the mountain, never really glancing anywhere else. The gifts on either side of the mountain or off in the distance remain unseen. But what if we focused on more than simply what we expected to see?

Around the mountaintop, birds are flying, and trees are growing. Underneath this sugarcoated mountaintop, life is beginning as it

---

[5]   "Expectation." *Merriam-Webster.com.* 2014. http://www.merriam-webster. com (7 January 2014).

readies for spring. The evidence of God and all His blessings sit below the surface. Deep beneath the mountaintops, the life that God creates is resting in lush beauty. But one who looks solely for the mountaintop sees only the mountaintop and is unaware, from a place of consciousness, of what sits beneath the sugarcoated surface. Both the beauty and the experience of it are ignored.

Why do we not look at the whole picture? The explanation is simple. Our task-oriented minds focus only on the outside and look for what they expect to see. They do not venture deeper, under the sugarcoating, where the genius of God shows His true colors as life.

Try to envision a mountaintop the way you always see it, and then with a close-up view, float down underneath the sugarcoating into the world of the life beneath it. Keep your eyes open, and hold no expectations. Wonder at the experience of seeing what unfolds for the very first time! Do this through not your ego's eyes but with the intentionality of shared eyes—God's eyes, shared by you.

An easy way to remember to change your focus is by recognizing that what you focus on expands. Redefine your focus. When you catch yourself with an expectation, look beyond it and around it, envisioning a greater reality. Ask God to direct your focus. This greater reality is seeing through God's eyes.

Stephen Hawking said, "When one's expectations are reduced to zero, one really appreciates everything one does have."[6] Reduce your expectations to zero. Let God direct your eyes to what He wishes you to see, and view the world from a new place. Once you do, you will come to avoid all expectations, knowing them as limiting. You will begin to see more beauty and peace than any expectation could ever give you!

---

[6]   http://www.great-quotes.com/quote/36540

CHAPTER 24

———∽∿⟋⟍⟋⟍∿———

On Quieting and Opening

"Watch the world one blossom at a time.
Fill up with My beauty."

Today's hustle and bustle of life can be so stimulating. On the streets of New York City, there is always something to delight the senses. The sounds of cars driving down the streets, police cars driving by with their sirens, people screaming and yelling, the wind, the bells ringing in the churches, and horns honking all at once will take over one's thoughts and mind. One sees all the bright lights of Broadway, thousands of people crossing streets, traffic lights and cars, colorful billboards, and video screens of news broadcasts—all at the same time. The odor of garbage fills the streets, and the smell of smoke fills the air. Walking past a flower shop offers the fragrance of roses on display. The feeling of moist air on the skin and the soft breeze of the ocean can distract one from other thoughts. With all these things taken together, it can be difficult to focus on anything, let alone one's own thoughts. I go to New York as a visitor, and I am amazed by how people learn to function in such an action-packed environment.

We all learn to adapt to the specific sensory stimulation that bombards us in our community environments. Learning to cope with this is another way we occupy our minds. Organizing our day and our time and performing household duties, work duties, and personal duties in the few hours we are awake is a challenge. What does it do to us? It forces us to exist in a "mind state" instead of a "heart state," or the state of pure inner essence. Many of us feel as though we have little heart time, and we spend a good deal of time trying to sort through things that have happened, things we have to do, and things we would like to see.

When we are young, we are sent to school to educate our minds. There is little in the way of education regarding our hearts at school. As students, we quickly learn that mind time is of the utmost importance and that good use of mind time often will be rewarded with high grades. If we daydream and address matters of the heart, we typically are redirected. We discover that only "mind time" is acceptable.

Soon after a student begins school, homework is assigned. Not only is the mind to be occupied all day long from 8:00 a.m. until 3:00 p.m., and sometimes longer, but also in the late afternoons and evenings, the student must complete assignments and study for exams. In between the studies and the projects required of students in the United States, family time, such as dinner, may occur. But this is over quickly, and the student goes back to homework, pursuing high grades and never really becoming present to this now moment.

Our system of education does little to encourage time for heart or Self. Many school systems do not support music and art programs; they consider them unnecessary. There is money in the budgets to create more exams to assess the students' education and to build larger buildings, but there is not enough money to promote music or creative programs. The education system in the United States and many nations has gone the way of the mind, thereby doing an injustice to the soul.

Being trained by society to be thinkers, we are all doers of the mind. We view our emotions and feelings as weakness. Busyness results in our neglecting matters of the heart. Marriages are failing—and divorces are rising—because relationships of the mind are hard to keep together. In a busy world of travel and instant gratification revolving around the mind, all relationships begin to suffer. The relationships of husbands and wives, parents and children, students and teachers, families, friends, and coworkers have become increasingly difficult.

Dealing with the mind full-time creates stronger egos. Merit is based not on "who you are" but on "what you are." Collectively, we form a country of strong egos; therefore, it is not surprising that the world has observed us at times in disbelief. It is a severe consequence that our country's collective ego is scorned and disrespected by other countries in the world. As a world leader, we are modeling our behavior in front of the world, and the egos of other countries grow to compete with ours. Our world is functioning in a very dysfunctional way, for operating totally from mind is heartless and lacks compassion.

We each need to quiet the mind so the heart can be heard. With all the mind noise that exists in the world today, it is not easy to know one's heart. As long as the mind is respected most, time to be who you are will only become clouded by the "what" you are in your life.

How do we begin to quiet our minds? How do we screen out the mind noise to let the God within our hearts shine through us to the rest of the world? In order to find that place deep within us—the place where God speaks, we must first learn how and when to employ our minds. Our minds have found a way to use us, and in the process, they gain heaviness and weigh down our hearts. This is the feeling of being "weighed down." This idiom is a feeling based upon a real spiritual happening. Our hearts get heavy. We cannot find them beneath the layers of untruths our minds have come to believe. Our minds were meant to be a beautiful resource capable of being put into action only when needed and to be rested at other times to allow us to feel the world, to enjoy our lives, to connect with God, and *truly to be*.

One can become aware by only using the mind for planning practicalities. Once one becomes aware, living in the present becomes the human state, while every moment is lived consciously, fully, and completely. The man-made concept of time becomes less important while the spiritual life of each of us is free to explode in wonder.

It has been said, "Life is for the living." A life lived through the mind is not truly lived because it is not felt. No wonder we don't feel joy or happiness! We spend our lives going from a past moment to a future moment. We walk here to get there. We do this so that won't happen. Many of our daily thoughts are about how to prevent something in the future from happening; it is as if we think we have the power to control our lives. How much energy is spent on trying to keep the status quo? Do we really control it? How many moments do we really *feel*? How often are we focusing on the present moment?

Our relationships are mostly mind relationships—one-dimensional and lacking consciousness and deep awareness. They are based upon ego—the armor that most of us wear—under the illusion of protecting our hearts. Our arguments and fights with our partners are always displays of ego. Hurt feelings result from one person attempting to attack another's layer of ego. The attacker's ego then becomes stronger.

Feelings of superficial love created by mind relationships are ego-strengthening relationships. Why do we choose to be with this lover?

Often, the answer is "because this person makes me feel good." This love has an opposite: we can decide that this person no longer satisfies us and that we dislike him or her. This is an ego dance. This is not about the pure love that comes from deep within us—an eternal love that has no opposite.

A relationship from one human being to another can be love without ego, leaving an opening for God's love to flow into it. There is another opening that forms when the shell of ego cracks. From deep within this fissure, the inner essence of being can finally be free to expand and breathe. Any opening can become a place where our hearts expand and God may create. Silence and stillness are two ways we can remain open to God in a present moment.

How often are you sitting *still* in the moment? How often do you sit, without anything to do, just existing on your chair? How often do you feel awareness of your body? Do you see the light as it falls on the walls opposite you? Do you smell the coffee in the coffeemaker in the kitchen? How about listening to the birds sing with all their wondrous voices in chorus? Spend some space and time sitting and listening with vigilance to the silence. The silence has its own sound. The space within it brings peace. Sit down for a moment to pause in the busyness of your life. Take a moment at work to look out the window. Let the silence touch the space within you. Sit down, and just *be*.

Sometimes you will find it hard to stop the flow of thoughts running through your head. If you absorb the present moment by using all your senses, or merely listen with awareness to the silence, your thoughts will cease. You can also make your thoughts cease by looking into firelight, or by looking up at the sky and focusing not on the clouds, but rather, on the empty space. This empty space, whether auditory or visual, will provide an instant "shut off" for your mind, ceasing thought. Silence or emptiness is within the deepest part of you, all the way down to the atom.

The Diamond Sutra, a Buddhist text, says, "Form is emptiness; emptiness is form." Relax and be with the emptiness, and you will become the emptiness. By doing this exercise for minutes at a time, you can stop the flow of thought, giving yourself much needed "recharging" time. This is only the beginning of a process that will take you much deeper. It will be where thought stops and experiencing God begins. It will allow a creativity of which you never knew you were capable. Every time you have a big decision to make or a big project to do, allow yourself to stop and take some space in the silence. Doing this when you feel overstimulated will help increase your creativity from a deeper space within you. It can become a space of great inspiration and a space of peace, love, and joy.

Most of us exist through the visual arena. We watch and look, but we rarely listen. Things that catch our attention are bright, flashy colors, beautiful sights, and awesome shapes. It takes something out of the ordinary for us to pause, stop, and listen. Only things like loud bangs and noises, particularly distinct sounds, and unexpected sounds catch our interest. The art of listening is just one of many things that is no longer important to our lives. We listen to main words when others talk—but not to the words in between. We try to get the "gist" of their thoughts. But sometimes the words in between carry the feelings and the intent of the utterance. Multitasking is the way we have learned to function, giving everything we do a little bit of our attention and awareness.

Once we really learn how to listen to silence, the forms that come out of silence become more beautiful to us. It is no different than if one is painting a picture on a canvas. When we stare at a canvas, it is white and empty. Our minds soon become still. Once a line is drawn on the canvas, we label it as art. All beautiful things are best appreciated from empty space. An art sculpture is placed in a room—usually alone—so it can be viewed within the emptiness that surrounds it. When we appreciate music, we listen to it uninterrupted, in the silence of that moment.

What things do you find beautiful in your life? Look upon the blueness of the sky. Notice that as a cloud begins to form it becomes more beautiful to you. The smell of a delicious dish in the kitchen is appreciated solely, not next to odors of perfume and garbage. A soft touch on your skin does not feel soft unless you feel it with full awareness. The taste of a food is often distorted if there is another taste in your mouth at that time. If you chew and swallow and empty your palate, you will be able to taste the exquisite flavors with awareness, one at a time.

Listening to silence can become an adventure. It will bring you an inner stillness. If you learn how to listen to silence, you will learn how to listen more carefully to what grows out of this silence. Just as clouds become more beautiful when they grow out of the blueness of the sky, everything becomes more beautiful when it grows out of the emptiness of silence. By doing this, and listening, you will forge a new pathway away from thought and into the realm of being.

As we learn to listen to silence, which is really empty space, we can begin to listen to what comes out of the silence: the sounds of trees swaying in the breeze, birds singing unique songs, frogs down by the lake, crickets in the grass, cars driving by, and voices speaking words. We seldom focus on what we hear. Instead, our obsessive thoughts lead to other thoughts. Before we know it, we are off on a tangent—when what we wished for was the experience of listening. This is what happens to each of us every day. We find ourselves in a world of thought while watching someone's lips move back and forth and sideways. What a useless exercise they are doing! They feel our disinterest and abandonment of their feelings! What is most perplexing is that this is not the intent for most listeners. Our wish is to listen, but our minds get in the way, thinking of all the things that catch our minds. Do you stop listening when you have questions so that you no longer hear the speaker at all? Do you only hear the question in your head? How can we say we are listening when this happens? Aren't we really thinking about our own agendas?

When one attains stillness from creating space for silence and emptiness, listening becomes a new and wondrous experience. We can listen not only with our ears, but also with our eyes and our hearts. We learn there is more to communication than hearing another voice. We awaken to the look in our friends' eyes, the expressions on our friends' faces, the body language our friends use while expressing themselves, and the intonation and pauses in their speech, which give us the understanding of what they are trying to communicate. Don't we miss a great deal just dealing with our own minds and keeping them at bay when someone is trying to communicate with us?

Take time out of your busy schedule for a break of space. Listen to the silence, and learn a new awareness. Let this space and silence be the canvas on which you paint your day. You will be surprised by how your job and your play will become a work of art and beauty.

CHAPTER 25

Finding Gifts within the
Storms of Chaos

"Chaos is My workshop.
Chaos is where I thrive.
Find Me in the center of the chaos,
and you will find peace."

L ife is going great. You are on top of the world! Your work is moving forward, and your family seems good. It appears that you have everything under control, and things are almost perfect. Then, one unsuspecting day, you wake up, and your once peaceful world turns into a hurricane: the basement floods; the car breaks down; health issues, financial issues, family issues, job issues, and legal issues all hit you at once! When the initial shock is over, the questions begin: *What's happening to my life? Why is everything is going down the drain? How can I keep centered in this chaos?*

Uncertainty always falls randomly from the skies, mostly when you think you have life under control. It follows the second law of thermodynamics: everything moves toward chaos. Your mind believes everything is in place, and then without warning, winds and fog block your view, creating chaos that becomes visible everywhere once the fallout clears. Your first reaction is to panic!

This wonderful work you have done to keep everything in place, striving to the best of your ability to meet every challenge, is ruined! How can you clean up this inconvenient mess? How do you find order amid turbulent winds that have not stopped blowing?

This mess is scattered everywhere, and the havoc is so dynamic that you cannot hold it still! Energy in chaos is not something you can control, and the fact that you can't control it is a reminder that life is not within human control. If you are lucky, you awaken to a greater reality—the reality that God is in control!

Our minds ask, "Why me? What have I done wrong? Why is my hard work being destroyed? What happened to my ability to control things?" These questions are based on the illusions with which we live. The most helpful and captivating question is "Who is trying to show me a greater truth?"

Will our minds allow us to focus in this new reality? Fruitlessly, they point to the task at hand, a futile endeavor of struggling to put things back into the same places they were before. How often we do this without recognizing that all of God's new creations begin with chaos!

I invite you to look at chaos in a new way. Accept the chaos. It is pointless to resist what already is. Make a conscious choice to be open to it.

In *Seven Life Lessons of Chaos*, John Briggs and David Peat say, "Artists, healers, and those undergoing life changes open up to the uncertainties accessing degrees of freedom that can spur new self-organization."[7] Have you tried opening to chaos? Have you tried to understand what it teaches you about yourself and about God? In chaos, God creates new growth. You can no longer do things the way you did them before, and you are open to new ways—ways that were closed to your mind when it did things by habit and thought everything was under its control.

"When you always do what you always did, you will always get what you always got." Do you see yourself in this quote? What if there are new possibilities for you? What if God wishes better things for you? How can you see while you are buried in your same routine, believing the illusion of control? Perhaps the greatest reality is that God is creating new, more wondrous possibilities for you!

If you find chaos in your life, and it feels frustrating to your mind, can you open your heart to it? Open your heart, and see chaos as the birth of new possibilities, new organization, and new growth deep underneath the fog. Let go. Walk toward faith by allowing God to do what God does—create change and beauty through chaos. The chaos of a storm cleans the trees of old debris and blows away worn and weak branches. When it's over, chaos allows that tree to bloom and blossom in a new and healthier way!

Inside each form of chaos is a lesson in letting go, beginning with illusions. We learn to let go of the illusion of control. At first, we find ourselves holding more tightly to what is not real—the untrue stories our minds create, thinking that if we hold on, we might find a way to control our environment. I invite you to awaken to a greater reality, the reality of a God much greater than the illusions of the human

---

[7]   F. David Peat and John Briggs, *Seven Life Lessons of Chaos* (New York: HarperCollins, 1999).

mind. Open to a greater freedom, beyond the mind's limitations that force us to hold to these illusions. Perhaps you will find within this greater reality a wondrous sense of opportunity and possibility! Perhaps, if you learn to accept and open to the chaos, you will be able to allow God to do what God does.

When, at last, the fog gently lifts, and you open your eyes in awareness, you will find a handful of God-given gifts from the storm.

CHAPTER 26

———✦——✦——

Creating Space

"All I ask of you is for the space for you to see Me.
I will create within the space you give Me."

I tell my students that part of their daily journaling is writing a list of what is on their minds before beginning a morning practice or meditation. When one empties the mind on paper before beginning the day, the mind prisons are emptied. The content being recorded on paper provides a record to which the mind can refer. One reason our minds revolve around and around is to keep within the short-term memory what they fear they may lose or forget. By recording what worries us or what needs to be addressed, the mind can let go of the future and rest. We can focus on the now moment, where the true Self grows and expands instead of the mind.

Before an important meeting with a client, peer, or friend, you can do the same thing. Taking a moment to allow the contents of your mind to be written down on a piece of paper or visualizing blowing it all away is a perfect way to empty your mind. It does not take long to wake up to how much you use your mind. Put it to rest by emptying it so it becomes lighter and allows for the expansion of the heart.

You will find that, from a place of lightness and emptiness, you will present to another person as being open. There sitting before this person is space that is open and willing to listen. For the listener, it feels as though time, heart, and undivided attention are focused on her. What environment could be more beautiful and comforting for a fellow human being?

Most of us listen from a place of filled space. Our minds are full, and we glance at our watches frequently while another person is talking. By these mannerisms alone, anyone coming to us in need may feel constricted. Voices get louder, and speech gets faster as this true Self tries to fit feelings into a limited space. With no time to talk and no place to air feelings, the other's heart sinks underneath an active mind. Feelings become harder to share when being concise is the focus instead of sharing the heart. Friends who come to you in need are given the task of saying what is bothering them with the hope that you will listen rather than *knowing* you will.

Which way would you rather someone listen to you? When you need quick answers, deeper listening may not be necessary. But there is so much to learn from deeper listening, and ideas flow more easily when you are open. You may learn that the answer "no" won't come to you when there is openness and the feeling of infinite potential. Innovative ideas are created from the empty space within the heart. Our minds are finite and only capable of what they already know. Our hearts are vast and creative, making it possible to access God's infinite qualities.

CHAPTER 27

The Freedom of Letting Go

"Free your Self from endless slumber.
Cut the ropes, for you are bound.
I have given you the freedom
to choose Me freely."

I remember the exact place on my walk where these words came to me. I was standing on a street corner, back to wellness but not back to life, erased of *what* I was, about to learn of *who* I was. As I walked down the sidewalks, I filled with love for the beauty around me, and I had a sense of my heart. I knew in that moment how pure it was and how loving and kind it was. God said, "Be the love; be the kindness to the world."

This was not quite so simple as decades of judgment resurfaced in my mind. I was a judger of my Self for every step of freedom my heart tried to take. I had always felt awkward in my life, trying hard to please others and finding it just was not possible. Now I see this so differently. I was allowing judgment to bind me, keeping me in line by insisting that I play by the rules. I felt caged in a structure of which I could not be free. Judgment—of myself, by others, and of others—was keeping me in a prison of my own creation.

The prisons we create are complex and multifaceted. Our minds build them to keep us away from our hearts. We become like mice walking around a maze. Beginning with the illusion of control, we live with the illusion that we are the ones who create outcomes in our lives. This fear-based illusion follows a pattern:

1. The human mind, due to its comfort in routine, removes the infinite choices we can make from the options open to us in the world.
2. This comfort—routine—becomes habit to us.
3. We allow our habits to dictate what we do, how we see the world, how we see our choices, how we see our options, and how we see our lives.
4. All choices are seen through the screen of the limited mind, only letting through limited choices.
5. We choose to see through the mind because the mind surveys possible dangers, and more often than not, sees the unknown definitively, making it easier to make decisions. Yet our minds see the unknown as limited and filled with only bad possibilities.

Although our minds gravitate toward this fear-based pattern, the heart sees the unknown with hope—as a field of infinite good possibilities. When we look from our hearts, or our Selves, we begin to realize the infinite possibilities of the present moment. We look at what we can do right now. We recognize that we can do what we always have done, or we can do one of the infinite things of our choosing. Can you list the things you might do at this moment that you never thought of before?

Habit is just that—habit. Our habits are based upon the routines that our minds created at various times in the past. Habits do not have to continue. Habits can be broken, but only if we see the infinite possibilities for things we can do in their places. Our minds do not take this extra step. Our minds tell us that habits create predictable outcomes. We stick to our habits because our minds tell us the outcomes will always be known, safe outcomes. But are these expected outcomes always what our hearts wish for?

We are afraid of the unknown, but why do we fear what we do not know? If there are infinite possibilities in the world, there are infinite good possibilities too! We have the choice. Why must we fear? Everything that exists in the world has infinite possibilities and infinite variables that can affect their existence or outcome. Our science is based upon predictability, yet experiments are done in a vacuum. Experiments are controlled. Life is not. Often, we rely on science to predict the outcome of a situation so we no longer have to fear a bad outcome. This is for our own comfort.

Why do we gain comfort from routine? Why do we not gain comfort from knowing there are infinite good possibilities and choose one of those instead? When did we learn to value predictability over the *adventure of possibility?* If we can make peace with the fact that there are no ironclad answers, that there is no one way to do things, and that there is no black and white, then perhaps we can break free from the prisons of our routines and see the world through God's eyes.

The next illusion we must face is the one of striving for perfection. We spend years of our lives walking on eggshells to try to avoid making mistakes. No matter how hard we try, the truth is that the mind is not capable of seeing perfection for long. It is only a matter of time before the mind finds a flaw—large or small. Our minds think it is their job to detect what is wrong in a given situation. How can a mind create perfection when its focus is on wrongdoing? Is this not a futile task? Our need to strive for perfection is an illusion. With a limited mind that sees only imperfection, perfection is never possible.

God made our hearts in His image. This is the part of us that is perfect. This is the part of us that was created to grow and burst through the soil to blossom. Our hearts are imprisoned by our heavy minds. We live in mind prisons, fearful of judgment. We spend our lives searching outside ourselves for the answers, never once realizing that our hearts hold the key!

Outcomes are ultimately not under our control. There is always a variable of grace. We rarely consider this variable. We have fooled ourselves into thinking we are in control of the outcomes. We live with the illusion of control, and when outcomes are not what we want, we blame others or ourselves. If we were to let go of blame and judgment—living instead from a free place inside, allowing God to do what God does—think of how much empty space we would have! If you allow yourself to think in terms of infinite possibilities, you will no longer feel trapped in your life.

Whether one is feeling judged by others, judging others, judging oneself, or letting go of the illusions of perfection and control, human beings are bound and imprisoned by their past conditioning. When we let go of all of these things, we are left with amazing freedom and incredible space to be creative, to let our hearts grow, and to love.

CHAPTER 28

A View from the Center

*"Every moment is a frozen moment in time
once you become aware of We."*

Can you remember your very first "God experience"? Have you ever had an experience of a beautiful moment, frozen in time? We are each called to God early in our lives. If you reflect upon your life, you can find these moments. It really didn't matter where you were, what you were, who you were with, or what you were doing. What mattered most was that you connected with the sacred within you.

Some call these "Kodak moments." They are picture-perfect times of feeling so "alive" and in touch with the purpose and value of one's life. We catch a glimpse of a greater reality from the moments when we feel so small in God's infinite universe. We "get it" for a nanosecond, sensing a deeper knowing that we are supposed to be here and that everything is as it should be.

Can we readily create these Kodak moments in our lives, and can we learn to live this way? Yes, we can! We do this by living from our hearts while seeing God in the center of everything around us and more. We simply go to the center of every single moment. That center is where God is. Within that God-center—the eye in the hurricane of life—we find peace.

In the center, where God resides, the peace of the moment resides. It is where we feel most aligned with the power of God and the wonder of life.

Going to the center means when you are planning the budget at work, you remember that you are a spark of God and become aware of the gifts of that moment. Though your mind computes away, your heart flows with the people around you. You remember to look deep into their eyes for the light of God. You weave words to the melody of their smile. You touch their hearts with your kindness and hope, becoming conscious of the center of the moment.

In a meeting room, look around you. Though your mind is working wildly on the subject at hand, your heart is looking for an opening through which to flow. And the words that come from your lips ride on a carpet of goodness and love. Your heart never sees another unkindly, and if a coworker speaks unkindly, you can feel that his heart is not at peace. If you are focused on the center, you can send your love and acceptance to that person's heart.

Living in the center means that when you stroll from your house or office to the car, you awaken to the beauty of the moment all around you. You not only glimpse it; you inhale it all into your heart and savor it. Looking at the fall colors, you realize that God is in the center of this beauty. A bird flies overhead, and you marvel at its powerful wings in flight. Waking up to presence, you can see God in action at the very core of life's miracle.

Most of us live as if we alone are the center of the universe—and the world revolves around us. Have you ever imagined yourself on the petal of a flower? Have you ever seen the world from the center? Our typical way of looking at life is from our ego's eyes. This is often the reason for our loneliness. See life from the center of the moment— God's eyes—with a new awareness of a greater reality!

Each moment you live in presence is a moment with God. Each moment of your awareness and consciousness of the center is a moment of joy and bliss—an eternally present moment! We can see the world's harmony with new awareness from this place, which is the brighter side of life! We are not the center of the universe. God is!

Make a vow to live your life differently than you ever have. Wake up to real meaning and purpose. Align your true Self by finding God in the center of the present moment, and you will begin to feel the experience of God! Connect with the sacred within you!

CHAPTER 29

―――⁓ꙮⓧ⊙ⓧꙮ⁓―――

Judgment Fills Up Space

"Your judgment of others is a waste of space.
Let Me be God."

W hen we speak about *being*, we speak about freedom: freedom *to be*, to live, to *choose* over and over again the same or different options in our lives. Nothing is as powerful as making a free choice based only upon feelings of love, compassion, and goodness freely flowing from your true Self, your heart.

Most of us find this most difficult to fathom. *Make a choice based upon only one's feelings? Why doesn't mind play a role? Isn't it selfish not to take into consideration the feelings of another? Shouldn't we be thinking of others before ourselves?*

From a spiritual standpoint, anything that comes from the heart is beautiful and should be shared with care and love. The honesty of loving freely is refreshing. The integrity in pure goodness bypasses conflict between mind/ego and heart.

There is only pure goodness emitted from the true core of being—our heart connection to God, our inner essence. What do we usually do? We make our decisions solely upon mind stuff. Much of our essential goodness, freedom to be, and liberation of choice is elusive, hidden under the heavy weight of the mind.

What other boulders are on our paths? The most impeding of all obstacles is judgment. Judgment restricts us and keeps us from going deep into the heart where goodness and love reside freely.

Three types of judgment interfere in the freedom to be: judgment of one's self, judgment of others, and judgment by others.

Look at your life situations. How many of your decisions are made to please others? How many are made due to anticipation of someone's judgment and your worry that the person will have bad thoughts about you? Which of your decisions reflect an "old judge" from your past who still haunts and conditions you? And how hard are you on yourself with the decisions you make? How much second-guessing do you do?

If you know well who you are beneath the shell of ego that is cracking slowly, you know the intentions behind your actions are always to do the right thing, to be good, to be kind, and to be compassionate. There is no doubt that if you didn't have the judgment of another with which to contend, you could see this more clearly and feel your own integrity. However, with the presence of judgment, integrity is compromised. Truth becomes elusive when decision-making is clouded by judgment. The heart is elusive when the mind takes over. Solutions become more difficult because you are bound by fear.

Is it possible that much of the space in your life is filled with fear of judgment? *What will my sister say if I tell her how I really feel? How could I live with myself if I were that selfish? What got into Sarah yesterday when she told her husband she wished to be free?* Judgment! All different shades of judgment! No freedom to be.

We have been conditioned all our lives to be untrue to our true Selves; we are taught to be careful about what other people think instead of listening to our hearts. Haven't we stopped being true to our hearts by listening to our minds? We have been taught to cover our feelings and hearts to protect them under the premise that our hearts need protection. So untrue! Our *minds and egos are protecting themselves*. Your heart is your greatest strength!

From this moment on, take a moment to reflect before you act on what you *think* in a present moment. Instead, stop to feel the beauty of that moment, and be those feelings. Look for the gifts, and put your focus there. Set aside ego, and let go of judgment—yours or another's. Use the basic love, goodness, and kindness inside you. Decide with integrity, and watch your heart blossom with love!

CHAPTER 30

—∿∿∽ᑕᔒᑐᓆᑐᓍᑐ∿∿—

The Story of the Garden

"I create from emptiness.
The Universe began from emptiness.
Look at a beautiful garden.
This, too, begins with emptiness—
one seed, one round seed, and emptiness.
Emptiness is necessary for a garden to bloom freely."

The beginning of Genesis speaks of the emptiness from which God created:

> In the beginning God created the heaven and the earth. And the earth was without form, and void; and darkness was upon the face of the deep. And the Spirit of God moved upon the face of the waters.[8]

Born from within simple emptiness and space is the world you see now, a world filled with the beauty and love that is also within us. All creation begins with empty space. The artist begins with a blank canvas, and from this empty space, he creates, sharing beauty and emotion from his soul. A carpenter begins with emptiness and a few pieces of wood. A composer requires silence and emptiness to create a melody that elicits feelings from deep within her soul. From nothing always comes something.

God works from emptiness within our lives. We cry out from the space within us when we feel lonely, asking God to create within the empty space. Death of a loved one leaves us feeling empty, and we ask God to create a sense of peace and aid us in our loneliness. Emptiness is necessary for creation—creation of new life within us and without.

When we create a simple garden, we, too, must begin with emptiness. We clear the soil of pesky weeds and debris. We turn over the soil to make sure it is empty so that roots will be able to grow without interference. We water the soil and give it nutrients so the garden will flourish and grow. It is important for the garden to have enough light and water, and when the soil is ready, we plant the seeds beneath it and wait for something to happen.

For what are we waiting? We wait for outward signs that the garden is growing, for we cannot see that new life has begun deep under the ground. Underground, seeds have cracked open, and their green shoots are already beginning to form small roots. Life has begun!

---

[8]   Genesis 1:1–2 (King James Version).

The garden is being created inside the ground. It will soon erupt and cut through the soil on the outside. It all began with emptiness.

The human mind sees emptiness in a different light. Our minds see emptiness as something missing, a place of lack. Because of this, as discussed earlier, we try to fill the emptiness with quick fixes and wants from outside of us. We buy things, we get busy doing things, or we seek things. At a certain point in our lives, we realize that we feel empty and that everything we did to fill the emptiness has left us feeling even emptier.

Our minds cannot understand the creation of beauty in our lives. Minds cannot understand beauty, for it is their job to dissect it and evaluate it but not appreciate it. If the mind sees an empty garden, its first thought is about how to fill it. It does not occur to our minds to allow God to create within the emptiness.

In a garden, the human eye cannot see what has begun inside seeds underneath the soil. In fact, while life is thriving underground, there is nothing on the surface of the garden. Although our eyes may look upon the garden every day, impatience may cause our minds to assume that the garden is not taking hold.

Is this garden's outcome really up to us? For what are we waiting? We wait for some visual indication that the garden is growing. For whom do we wait? We wait with patience for God to create a masterpiece. The outcome of this garden is up to God. Thinking we are the ones creating the garden is an illusion we believe—a lie our minds created. But if we sit with patience, we can realize that a garden is life and beauty that God is creating.

To appreciate the beauty of a new creation from within the heart, we need space within us to grow, coupled with vigilance or awareness. With continued patience, we open our eyes to signs of growth; if we are busy, we might not see them. In the space of awareness, within weeks, we will see the green sprouting of seeds beginning to grow above the soil.

With patience and awareness, we watch the fragile patches of green as they appear all over the garden. Every day we visit the garden, we see what has begun to cut through the soil and grow. We can do this on the surface of our being, or we can see it with the eyes of a child, taking it deeply into our hearts. With wonder, we are able to feel and observe the creation of life and feel the beauty God has given us.

How do we assist God with this endeavor? Through awareness, we learn what the garden needs. We guard the plants from too much sun and from life forms that may hinder their growth to keep the blossoms healthy and strong. When the summer sun becomes too hot and dry for the flowers to open, we know they need water. With patience and awareness, we try to be flexible with these life-sustaining tasks—collaborating with God to create the most beautiful blossoms. Flexibility is necessary for the growth of any new creation.

How does our garden really grow? It grows with space, patience, awareness, and flexibility, but the most important variable in all creation is surrender. Without surrender to our God to create life within the garden, no seedlings would sprout. While we remain patient and aware, watering the garden and being flexible enough to know when it needs our attention, we wait for God to create and surrender the outcome to Him.

This garden is a metaphor for our spiritual lives. The world today is filled with things to do and ways to be. Our inner selves are saturated with thoughts and doings, but we do not find the space to nurture our inner gardens. We allow weeds to fill it, leaving little space for the blossoms and new seeds to grow deep inside the soil. We think we have control over the garden, and we allow our minds to forget that this is an illusion. True control is the variable that is up to God. Space, patience, awareness, flexibility, and surrender are all necessary for our inner gardens to grow.

We need to find the space for patience in this creation. Our world is filled with quick fixes and instant gratification to fill us. However, gardens do not grow this way. Seeds cannot sprout instantly, and a fertilized egg does not grow into an infant instantaneously. In this day of instant gratification and text messaging, God's creations do not happen as quickly as our minds think they should.

Your spiritual life is a joint effort between you and God. The seeds God planted within you are meant to grow. If there is no space or emptiness, there can be no growth. If you have no patience, you will not see the new green cut through the soil. If you are unaware, you will miss the blossoms of the flowers. Flexibility is important to care for the needs of each plant and to surrender to God, who creates the life within the garden walls.

Deep inside each of us are seeds that were planted long ago by God. If we allow for the space and emptiness, the seeds can begin to sprout. With space, patience, awareness, flexibility, and surrender, our inner gardens grow. The space in the garden allows the freedom to be and grow wildly; the colors of the flowers express love from the Infinite through their beauty.

Look at your life. Do you allow the space for the garden of your heart to grow?

CHAPTER 31

—⚬⚬⚬⚬—

The Two Worlds

"You are asleep to My greater reality.
Wake up and see your infinite nature—
We."

My journey took me to a world of which I had never been conscious before. The most fascinating part of it is that it was always in front of me, but my mind was so focused on doing the tasks it had planned that the simplest things had been overlooked. I realized this is why some people do not believe in or even have a sense of God. They become analytical about what is in front of them and lose the grandness of the infinite picture. They focus on the complicated, trying to decipher it—a mind task—instead of focusing on the simple, which is reality. When one has "stuff to do," the birds in the trees can wait until later. When one's mind is wrapped around a problem, it seems almost silly to be wondering what the inside of a flower feels like. This world that seems perfectly simple—the essence of life itself—is elusive when one's mind is "doing its thing."

After I journeyed on, how clear it became to me! It is as though I had been looking at the wrong part of an optical illusion, mistaking my mind's will for the truth. I had lived in a dream world of stories until the simple truth of reality struck me. Then I made a paradigm shift.

Once upon a time, there were two worlds. One world was "heaven on earth." It was a world of reality, perfection, God, peace, and love. When one awakens to this world, and the sun rises, a picture is painted on the clouds. The birds fly from their nests to get food and almost dance through the air. Their early morning voices are filled with love and excitement about a new day with one another—a new day filled with opportunities to sing and to be.

The crows wake up early at dusk, flying toward the east; they find the highest tree in which to perch, and they speak in excited voices. When the sun finally begins to rise, the voices quiet, and all that is left to be seen are their shadows on the tree limbs as the crows watch the sky. The trees stand tall, and through connected God-consciousness, they observe the unfolding beauty. Filled and surrounded by the beauty of infinite green, they stand in majesty, sway with the breezes, and bend flexibly with the storms. Nothing shatters them as their consciousness is always with God and the sky—the symbol of life.

When a conscious human being rises to this world, greeted by the magnificence of a sunrise, he watches the sky mural in its wondrous colors and feels this gift from God. With peace in his heart, a man begins his day from a place of feeling God's love and joy, with kindness and goodness that was planted within his heart at the time of his birth. Each present moment brings infinite gifts to this man: the color blue in the sky above, the iris blossoms unfolding in glorious purple color, the grass swaying with the breeze. These gifts carry great meaning and are cause for wonder to be noted as gifts of love from our Creator. These gifts, when shared with others, create light—a spark burning wildly into a fire of glorious love.

The other world is one of "more." A less conscious man, awakening at the exact same time of day, jumps out of his bed, fearing that he will be late to work. If he is late, he will not make the money he needs in order to pay for the new car he purchased a month ago. Of course, his son needs to get those fancy sneakers all the kids at school have, so the man will need to work until late tonight. The sun rises, unnoticed, as this man continues his daily routine. The deadline for the project he is working on is Monday, and he fears telling his wife that he will be working through the weekend that she had hoped the family would spend together. He leaps into the shower, jumping out almost as fast because he must quickly shave and comb his hair. He races off without breakfast, driving quickly on the highway to his job, and hits a squirrel on his fast-paced way. Feeling a pang of sadness that he quickly forgets, the man continues on the road without looking back and without feeling what he left behind.

The most unbelievable part of living consciously is that one realizes everyone who lives for tomorrow or in the past is living within a story. Their stories are fantasies that their minds create. There is no truth to their stories: what has happened in the past is no longer the truth we experience now, and what will be in the future is not being experienced now. The only reality is the now moment and what our consciousness observes about that now moment. Once we judge it, perceive it, or think about it, it becomes a story we create. Many people walking down the street are not living in the present moment. Often, they are trying to live where they are going and ignoring now. While they walk, they may not feel the ground underneath their feet. They may not smell the freshness of the air or hear the birdsongs in the trees. Thinking of what will be when they arrive at their destination is simply a lie the mind creates; it is not reality.

Most people walk within their bubbles of perception, never knowing that the world of God is surrounding them. They believe these stories the mind creates are reality. Their responses to these stories are based upon this unreality. What happens as a result of their responses becomes distorted and, often, untrue. When we live in the past or the future, within the mind's stories, we are lying to our true Selves.

There are two worlds as clearly as there is a flipside of any coin. Both are within your sight and within your heart. The world of reality and presence is God's world—the Kingdom. The other world is man's world.

God's world, or the world of reality, is one of love, faith, hope, compassion, peace, goodness, and joy. It is a world of beauty and a world of infinite potential. Man, in this world, sees life with the eyes of a child. Life situations are merely transient clouds in the sky to this man, passing through but never staying. This man realizes the beauty of a sunset, the peace in silence, and the joy in love. These feelings that he has and cultivates have no opposites, nor do they get covered up in mind stuff or have tos. They are what he lives for. They are the purpose of his life, and the things he does in God's world are done from a place of heart. He *visits* man's world because his home is anchored with God in reality. He employs his mind to do a task, but he lives from his heart.

The other man, the one whose life is run by life situations and perceptions, is blind to God's world. He spends his days worrying about the future or regretting the past.

Most of us live in man's world. There, we cling to our stories, which are unreality, and rush through our days. We live for future moments that we think we can make happen if we work hard enough, never realizing that the outcomes of our work are not up to us. In truth, they rely on a deep element of grace.

God's world has been hidden to us since the early days of our conditioning. As babies, we were born into God's world. We each arrived with an exquisite gift from our Creator—the spark of life and connection to Him in the God center, deep within us. As we grew into toddlers, our heart centers awakened inside us. We saw life through the eyes of a child, God's eyes. We saw the world through the eyes of infinite potential and beauty, and things that caught our eyes enchanted us. We did not analyze what we saw; we only loved it, were in awe of it, and honored it as sacred. When our minds awakened to the expectations and conditioning of man's world, we began to put layers over the world that God created.

Our parents conveyed these layers of conditioning to maintain an illusion that the heart needs protection. This blocked our access to God's world. Rules were made, and structure was formed, covering the world of the heart—God's world—in thick layers of untruth, never to be uncovered again.

Throughout childhood, as we grew and were conditioned further, man's world became more apparent. We saw models of behavior in society that illustrated what should be important to one who is growing into adulthood. As older children, we watched parents living and working to obtain things from outside themselves instead of modeling the importance of what is within, and this gave us a very strong message. We learned that we must get things from outside ourselves to complete ourselves. Most on this path felt pulled by God from time to time, experiencing pangs from the heart of love, traces of compassion, and semblances of joy, but these moments were few and far between.

One of the greatest illusions with which we live is that what is outside of us will complete us and that any discomfort of emptiness inside of us is to be filled with "things." From school age onward, we try to get things from the outside, including more things than others and intelligence instead of wisdom. All the while, we add layers of untruth and create an ego shell thick enough to block out God's world so that man's world becomes all that matters.

Occasionally, we awaken to God's world as it burns through thoughts, stories, and structure, and we have a day of incredible insight into reality while living in the present moment. Then, covered up once more with stories, structures, schedules, and the habit of buying things, we fill the emptiness again. These awakenings are little tastes of the world we left behind in the days of childhood—and little reminders to us that this world of God is still there. For deep within us, if we only burn through the layers that we have come to believe, we find the reason for being. This is enlightenment, or the Kingdom of Heaven, in all its beauty and simplicity then so easy to see.

Loneliness continues as one ages if a person remains in man's world. There, one's feelings of fulfillment are transient, because man's world is transient. This world comes and goes. God's world is eternal, as it reflects the qualities of God—the love that has no opposite, omnipotence, eternity, omniscience, wisdom, and the Infinite. This ever-present world of beauty creates rich, harmonic feelings that are painted in the colors of the world.

So how does one find God's world? enlightenment? the Kingdom? By seeing through the eyes of a child—with the eyes of space where these feelings and harmonies originate. By living in the present moment and knowing it is the only reality. The space within us and the space outside of us are just part of the infinite space of God. We each were given keys to this Kingdom. It takes an inner search to find it, but this search can be started immediately—right now, in the present moment—always. That is where this world is, and that is where God is.

The emptiness you feel was meant to be there. It was meant so you would feel and hear God and the world of the present moment in all its wonder and beauty. It is rather simple. However, when your mind hears this, it will try to talk you out of it. The mind fears emptiness. Many of my students say to me, "If it has been this simple all along, I feel as though I wasted my whole life trying to do things that did not matter." This is not truth. You have not wasted your whole life. You are meant to be here. It has all come to this: this truth, now, this revelation. You have arrived here, at the edge of the Kingdom of Heaven, by the grace of God, our Creator.

For me, doing this was not easy, and for a while, it was very confusing. There were times of conflict when I sat between the two worlds, not fitting into either. I realized that man's world—the world in which I had functioned my whole life—was a world of the mind's stories and illusion. Sometimes I didn't fit into the new eternal world, or God's world. I caught my mind attempting to take me backward, attempting to stay in charge where it was more comfortable doing what I always did.

I learned most of all that our place with God was to anchor in His world and only to visit man's world—to be *in man's world but not of it*. When Jesus described the Kingdom of Heaven, He described it in such a fashion. We are to wake in God's world and anchor in reality—the place of peace and the world of feelings—each morning. We are to hear His voice and His guidance. We are asked to fasten our true Selves to His world and take that world of God with us into the world of man. In this way, we bring the peace of God to the world of man. The other way, we bring the angst of man's world into God's Kingdom.

From God, I learned of the two worlds and how they do not combine into one until we learn how to see them both clearly. Once we do, and we see the contrast between the two, we realize that the way to master what we wish for is to focus on it. Whichever world we focus on grows.

Where do you wish to focus? Do you wish for a reality of peace and love and wonder? Or do you wish to focus on the stories your mind creates about what may come and go? What you focus on grows and expands. Focus on God's world, and you will have the keys to the Kingdom. Then watch it expand.

CHAPTER 32

—⁓∿⦅⦆∿⁓—

On the Elusiveness of God

"This is a journey of inverse thinking.
Whatever you think,
I am not."

In creation, from nothing—the emptiness—came something. And from God's something, man built layers and layers that covered God's creation and forgot the very essence of who we are—God-consciousness in human form, becoming aware of its true Self.

The human journey began from the simple, and as time passed, layers of thought were constructed to create things for use and function, making our journey more complex. We found things to help us care for ourselves, and we made tools with which to hunt for food. We invented more tools with which to eat, and tools with which to create homes and make clothing. More and better tools soon came, and with these, more and better clothing—the beginning of "more" and more things—more complexity!

Layers of clothing soon accompanied layers of thought. We learned to use our thinking to find ways to make better and better "things." Early tools became refined. The theme of "better" prevailed, and better thought produced better things, while more thought provided us with more things. Layers and layers added to the emptiness and nothingness as which we all began.

Soon enough, it was not only "better" and "more," but "more than this" and "better than that." The human mind worked to make life even more complex. Comparison became part of the human condition. We began searching for better things. Our reverence for what is in the present moment was replaced by a desire to live in the future, which was coupled with the concepts of more food, more clothing, better homes, and better tools. The mind became obsessive in the forefront, and the simple was no longer good enough and no longer in the spotlight. Although spiritual at first, the mind grew larger and heavier with more and more knowledge.

More knowledge brought more thought and less space. In fact, we began filling up the space with things that were not in the present moment. These things did not exist in the past or future. The small space of now, though in reality infinite, was covered up with lies.

Lies? Why lies? The future was just speculation—a story—and the past was over and done with. Yes, we required tools with which to eat and hunt. Yes, we required them to make clothing and to build.

Why are these lies? The future and the past take us away from the simple. They take us away from the truth—the present moment. In other words, the future and the past take us away from God.

When the mind is in control, it limits us. Because it cannot see the Infinite, it does not see the possibilities it has not experienced. These are possibilities that come from the Infinite—the innate union between God and us. We make decisions based upon what we know to be true, yet there are other things we have not tried that can be solutions too. These possibilities never enter the mind. It is set it its ways, using the same solutions that seem to work, over and over again. We continue to repeat this "structure" that the mind has created, taking the same way out every time. By doing what we always did before, we keep out the infinite possibilities that the world of God offers us.

Our minds are limited. We can hold only a certain amount of information before becoming overwhelmed or losing our memories. Our minds only know what they have been taught, what they have read, and what other minds have told them. Their very nature is limited. And being limited, they cannot hold what they do not know to be true. They do not hold what they have not seen, read, witnessed, or been told. Limited in what they know, they see the truth in terms of this paradigm. In reality, there is another paradigm with infinite possibilities that the limited mind cannot hold.

All the complexity that the human mind has developed was devised to take us far from the truth of who we are. Our minds have come up with a fantastic and foolproof way to keep God out. By making the world as complex as possible, human beings are unaware of their union with God and of the truth that God is inside them. We stumble through structures and complexity to find the "secret" that will give us inner peace. We find a web of form and structure, requiring use of our minds to find the way out. The mind, which is meant to be a tool, has devised its own trap to keep one within its confines, but the way to God is much easier than that. It is found within the simple. It is found within our being.

The essential secret being kept by your mind is how elusive God can be. You cannot feel God while simultaneously being deep in thought. The mind covers your heart with heaviness, keeping your thoughts revolving in the mind prison. Your consciousness of God is not found there. The only way to feel God is to set your mind free and experience Him through your heart. It is the journey in inverse thinking because your mind tells you that it takes using your mind to find your way to God.

It takes heart to feel your way to God. It's as simple as that. Once you feel God inside you, you know you are being led to a world of beauty and love. This world is absent from thinking; it is just as one part of an optical illusion is absent when you focus on the other. When you focus on thought, the experience of God is elusive to you.

Many spiritual authors speak of unlearning before one can experience God. What they are speaking to is the filled mind and its hold on us. Until we realize that what we know in terms of intelligence does not lead us to God, we are on a crooked path. Intelligence is obtained from the outside. God is found on the inside. God is found in the inverse of what one would think. This is the journey of inverse thinking.

CHAPTER 33

On the Stories We Create

"Always know the truth—what is—right now.
Truth is."

When journeying with God, I learned some powerful lessons. Many of them were about my relationships with others. I found that sometimes my relationships caused me undue pain, and I wanted to know why I was suffering so.

I asked God one day, when I had a particularly difficult challenge with a coworker. I constantly found myself in conflict with Leo. He said ambiguous things to me, and I went home and tried to decipher what he meant. I thought I knew what Leo was telling me from my own perception, or my own piece of truth, and when I did not know what he was talking about, my ego created stories about why he said the things he did.

God shared with me that I create stories about what people tell me. When there is not enough information, I soon realized, my mind completed the stories with its own agenda—usually something that made me fearful or caused me to suffer. I realized that this suffering was unnecessary. My mind did not understand why certain people did things, and it was merely guessing and choosing a story that was most uncomfortable for me.

It occurred to me that my stories were not the truth. This was a huge realization. My perceptions were not the truth, yet I saw them that way. I realized in a very real way that my mind lies to me. All this time, I had believed everything it told me was the truth. A huge paradigm shift was necessary. I learned to stop believing everything my mind told me. Instead, I started to believe what my heart told me.

Once we become aware of our perceptions and stories, we realize these lies are covering space we could be giving to God. The minute we stop listening to the stories we create, we become liberated from our obsessive minds. This is a pivotal moment.

From God's teachings, I now realize how we avoid connecting with one another from a place of heart. We live in worlds of lies. We walk around in our own worlds, with our own outside perceptions, and inside us is a heart that knows that truth is *now*. Truth is what we see in this moment. And the truth within another's heart can be found by sharing your heart. A simple question to another, such as "What do you feel about this?" or "What is in your heart right now?"

shows a caring and a patience that is needed to communicate the truth and not another mind story.

Let go of the stories you create about things you don't know. Let go of the stories you create about people whose hearts you do not know. The stories are simply lies your mind creates. Instead, take the time and the space to listen to someone's heart.

CHAPTER 34

On Finding Our Way Back When We Stray

"Our path together twists and turns.
I am the beacon in your soul.
I am home to you."

It is funny how the experience of God fades as mind situations come passing through life. Picture this: all of a sudden, you find the path veering into the greenery so that you do not know where to place your feet. If you walk straight ahead, you might miss a detail your mind feels is important, so you veer off the path and stumble into the woods.

As you walk off the path, the sun is slowly veiled from your sight. The sky fills with clouds, and the world darkens. It is then that you must watch your feet very carefully, for the mind tells you there are fearful ends you will meet if you step here or step there. As the woods darken, your eyes can no longer see the path you left behind. Sometimes it feels as though there is no turning back and you never will find your way back to God. The mind magnet pulls harder, showing you the crisis from an imminent point of view. Feeling that there is no other choice, you are limited and bound to this walking, putting one foot carefully in front of the other rather than skipping, jumping, and flying through the air as your heart so loves to do.

The path you left behind was bathed in sunshine, blue skies, and warm breezes. There was a gentle flow in that moving forward; it sometimes involved climbing uphill and sometimes involved strolling pleasantly past the most wondrous of colors. Leaving this path behind you results in every step becoming a hardship, a decision to imprison your soul. As time away from the path continues, the chains upon your arms and feet make you weary and exhausted.

Why do we leave the path behind us from time to time? Why do we lose the *present moment*? The answer is so simple yet so profound: because we have to lose our way to find our way. If we do not find our way back to the greenery with consciousness, we cannot remember how to get back on our path and stay there.

Every time we return from losing consciousness of the present moment, we learn more about what we allowed to take us away from God. The "acting out" of the ego often brings us to an unhappy or uncomfortable place. Sometimes it is greed or not listening to God as needed. Other times, it is knowing we did something very well and allowing it to go to our egos.

Reflection is necessary to find where we strayed off the path and to see clearly the illusions in which we were caught up. Spending some of your morning practice time reflecting on the life situation that took you away from the path is often needed to realign with the path. Use this time to look for important lessons that were learned in this process. These lessons can be meaningful further along in your journey. Reflecting is really backtracking, and it can be the most valuable process for increasing conscious awareness of the trappings that keep us from the freedom of being and the transformation that can occur within our lives.

When you lose consciousness of the present moment and the presence of God, the first step is to recognize that you have veered off the path. This consciousness of knowing is the awakening of the true Self and the observer. A simple glance at beauty through these eyes can burn through the layers that your ego has created between the true Self and the world of God. Watching this beauty, beholding it, and nurturing it is the key to the Kingdom of Heaven. Always bring your Self to God—the center of creation, the center of beauty, and the reason for being.

How do we find our way back to the path of presence? We do so by finding the center. We look for the light gently shining on the infinite leaves of endless greens. We look for the deepest color in the rainbows. We glance toward the sky and remember its light. God is always in the middle of all these beauties. God is at the center, and God always calls us back to the path when we have lost our way.

"You have to lose your way to find your way" has always been my mantra. With awareness, one learns many new and valuable lessons—some of great depth and meaning. The key is to know that when you are lost, you will be found by the beauty, by the center, by God.

CHAPTER 35

On Our Separateness

"It is only your ego that keeps you from Me.
If you feed it, you will be separate.
If you feed your heart, We will be united."

As we journey through our lives, many begin to feel emptiness. This feeling of lack or something missing is a sure sign we are being pulled by God to move deeper into our hearts. In truth, our essential purpose is to walk hand in hand with God as one, in conscious union with only one will between us.

Emptiness is the space where the heart expands. It is dependent upon our sense of true Self, which is connected with God within us. This true Self is filled with God's gifts to us. The will of our hearts, or our destiny, is aligned with God's will and the present moment.

The mind labors at creating and sustaining thoughts and perceptions according to its need to self-perpetuate. With thought comes the "mind's will" (one's perception of one's will), which is based upon our sense of self, or ego. This will is dependent upon things outside us to come to us.

In this world of form and things, there is much that weighs down our hearts, leaving little chance for God to rise up into our lives. If you picture a body of water, whether it is a lake or the ocean, it is easy to envision a heavy rock pressing down any life form. The rock is a metaphor for your mind and your ego; the life form is God within you and the gift of life He gives you.

A mind would say, "Well, God is capable of the infinite, so why can't He escape the heart and enter a heavy mind?" And from a mind place, that makes perfect sense. But the mind is limited, and God is infinite; God cannot fit into a limited space. Human beings have devised the perfect way to keep God out. We do so by staying in our minds and weighing down our hearts. You have been there when you feel "burdened," or "weighed down with thought," or with "a *heavy* heart." It happens to us when we push our hearts deeply down with loaded minds, not realizing from where we are making our decisions. Our minds become overactive feeding the ego.

The ego feels a great sense of itself. This ego keeps us motivated to continue doing what we are doing because we feel a sense of success, but as we continue doing so, we begin to lose touch with our hearts.

Over time, getting what we want fills the mind while pressing down the heart and trapping it deep underneath. As one's heart feels it wishes to be free from the burden, it begins to wish for something different. Individuals feel as though what they are doing is not bringing about feelings of satisfaction or desired outcomes. This feeling is the heart speaking of its wish to be free.

In *Eight Mindful Steps to Happiness: Walking the Buddha's Path,* Bhante Henepola Gunaratana said, "It is said that there are only two tragedies in life: not getting what one wants, and getting it."[9] Wants are the mind's desires. These desires cover the heart and keep us from the heart's wishes and desires. The things we want are always desires from outside of us, and they are dependent upon other people or other variables to materialize. They do not originate within us, nor do our hearts have any function in the outcome. We travel down a "mind path" to have these things for our very own. Our egos feel a sense of self when we obtain them, creating "separateness" between our minds and God's wish for us (our destinies). These are transient, though, as wants go by the rules of the world of form and its passing nature.

Our wishes are quite different than our wants. They originate from within us—deep inside our hearts. Wishes are always aligned with God and our heart's journey. Wishes can be present from the time of childhood and can come to fruition at any time in our lives when our hearts are uncovered. When a wish comes true, it is not of a transient nature, as a wish will lead one closer to heart and God. There is no separateness to a wish. When one wishes for something, God speaks through his heart. He and God are one.

Are you choosing to be separate from God? When you function from the mind and ego, ego is heavy and smothers your sense of God. When you function from the true Self, heart becomes light and floats to the surface. You and God are aligned, united, and without separateness. You walk as one, you feel as one, you choose as one, and you live as one.

---

9   Bhante Henepola Gunaratana, *Eight Mindful Steps to Happiness: Walking the Buddha's Path* (Somerville:Wisdom Publications, 2001).

We allow our wants to separate us from God and our hearts. We allow a transient purchase or temporary gain to be the reason for our lives. But when we live from our hearts, wants and desires are merely that—and they are known for their transient nature. We do not wait for them to fill us up, nor do they satisfy us. We have an awareness of the importance of the emptiness we feel within our hearts. It does not go unnoticed. We learn that if we become aware of it and walk through it, this emptiness will bring us closer to God and His infinite gifts. We have an inner knowing that emptiness is there for a reason. It belongs to God and brings us closer to God.

Your heart cannot expand and rise to hold the Infinite if it is trapped by a heavy mind. Keep your mind empty, and keep it light. Allow the heart to rise with the *unmanifested*—the gifts from God— love, peace, joy, faith, generosity, gratitude, compassion, kindness, and goodness. Then, you will have much peace and goodness to share with the world. These will become the gifts that, with consciousness, you give to the world from God within you. This is the magic carpet on which your deeds ride. This is the essence of your being—the God within you—shared with the world.

CHAPTER 36

Choose God

"You choose always outside of yourself.
Choose Me.
I am inside you.
Choose Me, and We shall never part."

Often, we catch ourselves with nothing to do, listening to our minds speak of boredom. Knowing there is so much on our plates, we feel stressed to perform, causing us to lose the precious present moment. This is what our minds tell us to do. We try to substitute now with have tos and want tos, using as an excuse anything that takes us away from the sacred space within us.

Sitting by your window, you can hear the beauty of a bird's song while it calls to show you what loveliness is singing this tune. You shake your head while urgently getting back to the computer as there is work to be done. Try to pull yourself away from that computer. Walk over to the window, look outside, and choose God.

Choosing God is as simple as holding a cup of warm liquid in your hands while marveling at its warmth. It can be as easy as watching the crows gather in the morning to celebrate the sunrise while you listen to the excitement in their voices as they chatter away. Choosing God can be finding the smile on a friend's face while beholding her beauty beyond the words, watching as her eyes dance when she speaks, and feeling deep love within your heart. Choosing God can be sitting with a sunset, even if it interferes with your plans for your favorite TV show, waking up earlier to light a candle in predawn and watching carefully as the flame blows in the breeze, gazing at a mountaintop and enjoying it even after the snow has melted, or watching each individual snowflake make a different choice for where on the ground it might land. If we let go of mind for a moment and choose God instead, the eternal presence of the moment shines through to us.

Choosing God allows us to take beauty-filled pictures with our minds and freeze these moments into our hearts. It allows us time to connect with the life of which we often lose track and to see the background of the picture. We have been too busy focusing on the life situations in the foreground.

This is the journey of inverse thinking—not seeing ourselves as things in space, but rather, seeing the journey as the space that connects our hearts and souls to the heart of awareness.

Choosing God instead of a planned event takes you outside the box in which you now live. Stepping outside of this box means opening up to the freshness of the world of infinite possibilities. Walking a path outside the box grows deep within you the spirit of adventure—the adventure of life of which we often lose sight. Life is not one damned thing after another; it is one beautiful miracle after another. It is all in the way you feel it when you choose God.

Perhaps one morning you will awaken to one simple voice within your heart asking you to go to the window. If you listen and choose God, a watercolor painting will be yours to experience.

Each morning, the splendor of sunrise heralds a new day, welcoming us to awareness of the present moment. Its beauty is a gift to all living beings, but those who move quickly from one life situation to the next do not experience the grace of this sacred moment. For whom is God painting this beauty-filled mural? Choose God, and you shall soon find out.

CHAPTER 37

*Freedom Is the Heart's
Most Basic Need*

"You have inner wings you cannot see. Use them."

Have you been there? Have you felt it deep inside you? You cannot seem to concentrate on anything for any great length of time, and you are no longer interested in things that used to drive you. Motivation is hard to find. You feel like a butterfly flying in circles or a car spinning its wheels. You have lost your way, and you have lost your purpose. Where have you been? Where are you going? Where are you *now?*

All of a sudden, your current purpose no longer fits your goals, and your future purpose remains to be seen. You feel like a spider spinning your own little web, catching yourself deep inside instead of prey. The world was once your playground, but lately, it has become a self-contained prison. Yes, you are restless.

Do you wait for a fleeting passion to catch your attention? Do you pause in front of the television and wait to become stimulated? Do you take your agitation out on your job, your wife, or your family? Would taking a college course help? Reading a new novel? Busying your mind? Would waking up tomorrow be any different if you weren't so restless? Chances are the answer to all these questions is a simple "no." May I suggest that your answers are merely right in front of you and outside your back door? Open up that door, and walk outside into nature.

There is a wondrous, beautiful world out there if you know how to focus on it and see it. Open up your back door and sit on that wooden chair in your yard. Open your eyes really wide and look out and up at the world. You are used to looking down by your feet, aren't you? Well, there is a world by your feet as well, if you look hard, and see without using your mind.

Restlessness comes from having too many scattered thoughts and not enough "heart time." It comes from being filled with energy that is no longer centered and focused, like lightning flashing through your mind. This raw energy comes into your brain and gets dispersed through your whole body, causing your legs to move, your heart to flutter, and your concentration to falter. Some call it being "bored," and others call it feeling disheartened. Actually, you are stimulated, but the energy is not collecting. It is being released before you have a chance to use it.

The cure for restlessness is to center yourself and become still. Stop what you are doing. Turn off the music. Turn off the TV. Put the book away. Sit still on a comfortable chair. If it is a cool day, put a blanket over your feet. Get comfortable while you sit. Stop being productive. Listen to the silence, and let the silence grow on you.

Within a few moments, you will be aware of the scattered energy throughout your body. Be present to it, feel it, and focus on it. Try to focus on the feeling of life coming from inside you. Do you know what I am talking about? In the stillness, feel the places in your body that feel the most restless. Those are the places! Listen to the silence, feel what energy is surging inside of you, and be present to it. Use your new awareness to feel your energy within the stillness.

Your life energy can always be a reminder of your inner essence and your connection to higher power. This higher power is stimulating your muscles to move and is forcing out the glow from within. Being restless can be described as feeling as though parts of you are glowing in the dark. But you want the energy to come from all of you—and from your inner essence, the soul of you, most of all.

Restlessness is a sign from the essence of your heart. It is as though your soul is saying, "Hey, I am here! Look at me! Remember me! Get in touch with me!" How can you hear it when you turn the music louder or surf the television channels? When we feel restless, our egos try to gain a sense of self by telling us that we are bored and have to fill the space. Our tendency is to listen to the ego and add stimulation. However, this is the opposite of what our true Selves need. Our hearts need space. While the mind craves stimulation, the heart we ignore wishes the inverse. It is there where we can obtain peace and serenity. If it were up to our minds, we would keep them busy all the time—functioning instead of feeling. We need to focus on the stillness and the life force inside us. We need to center ourselves and find ourselves.

Restlessness is a sign of your mind's inability to remain in presence, or in the state of now. Why do I say that? If you cannot resolve something now for the future, and you cannot change the past, you are forced to put your attention on this moment. Your mind does not like that. It wants to be solving problems and working overtime. When there is nothing you can do with the current situation, your mind does not know what to do. You move incessantly, trying to come up with problems to solve and tasks to begin—anything so your mind has something into which to sink its teeth.

But the reality at that point is that there are no tasks to be done right now. You might be asking yourself, "Why can't I relax?" In truth, your mind is controlling whether or not you relax. Who is in control of your body? You or your mind? How can you best use the time? Is it not an obsessive use of the mind to keep using it even though there is nothing productive for it to be doing?

Have you ever been bored and turned off the TV? Some call the silence deafening. It is the space in the silence that our minds fear—the emptiness. The mind wants to produce in this space, yet it is within this space that peace resides. The purpose of the mind is to use it when you wish to use it. The mind should not fill up all your space and cover your true Self. Your mind is merely a tool that you can use, if you so choose, to get things done.

In order to recharge and find your energy, you must touch the energy flow from within you. When you are bored and restless, do the inverse of what you have done before. Filling your mind more is not the answer. Find space, and you will feel freedom from the mind—a freedom that will bring you peace.

CHAPTER 38

—◦◦◦◦◦◦◦—

On Our Differences and Harmony

"You were created to blossom and grow in your infinite beauty,
and like the trees,
to sway together with the breezes."

You only need to walk through the airport before a flight and cast your eyes around to see the myriad differences in all of us. There are those with blonde hair, brown skin, red skin, rounder, slimmer, taller, shorter, and the list goes on with infinite possibilities. Some people wear colorful clothing and plentiful jewelry, others have tattoos, and some choose to be simple or blend in with others. Each of us, an extraordinary being, has a uniqueness that defines us in a way that is fascinating and miraculous. We are all different, yet surprisingly, we are all the same.

It is said that 99.99 percent of our genetic makeup as human beings is identical. This is incredible when we feast our eyes on the world around us. In a world that looks for differences to define us, we are all very much the same. Our egoic minds will not let us see our similarities—our unity. Minds are the policemen judging our differences as flaws. Yes, we look at our uniqueness as defects, and we do not see our differences as creating the beauty of humanity standing before us.

When we look at a wondrous garden, the flowers are each unique in color, shape, and size. It is the way the flowers flow together that brings to our hearts the gasp of beauty at what our eyes behold. If we were to look at a garden with only one kind of flower—all the same size, shape, and color, our eyes might be satisfied, but our hearts would not rise to the beauty before us. We would simply look away from this garden without comment. However, when we come to a garden with rows of uniquely different flowers, we stand in awe at the way they blend together in perfect harmony and beauty. We call this "breathtaking," for it takes our breath away. Our hearts beat in a new rhythm to this beauty—the consistent rhythm of God's love.

We are different, yet we flow in unity. When we are diverse in activities and interests, we are beautiful in our own ways. Shining the light of God from within our hearts unites us. The light of God connects us. Whether we know it or not, this is what is the same about all of us. What is similar about us unites us; our diversity becomes God's beauty and harmony.

What our egoic minds focus upon grows larger, and our minds want to focus on our differences rather than our center. We have been conditioned to use these differences against each other. Our differences come between us, and we use them as excuses for wars and disputes. Instead of looking at the beauty created by these differences in the garden of humanity, we look to these differences as being the problem with humanity. Groups of similar people find ways to isolate and avoid those perceived to be different, and prejudices are created. The beauty of harmony is lost to the whims of the egoic mind.

If we were to see our differences as the beauty in the garden of humankind, and to revere them and honor them in the true light of God's unity, they would be what we all hold in the center of our being—the seeds for peace among us. For then we would be viewing each other with the inclusive eyes of the heart—God's eyes—instead of the dividing eyes of an unforgiving egoic mind, or false self. The false self knows nothing of the garden; it knows nothing of unity and beauty. Its job is to analyze, compare, look for more, and judge that which is less. Its job is judgment, as if there were no God, His unity, or a greater reality. However, the false self, or ego, has no place as a judge in God's garden.

Harmony is beauty. Judging our differences unravels our threads. If we are to be a tapestry of color and beauty, we must learn to thrive together. We must see our differences as strengths rather than weaknesses and focus on what unites us. When we weaken those threads, we become weakened individually and collectively, and the vision of the garden unravels. We are God's united garden of humanity—wondrous colors united in Him. Why do flowers bloom in this garden? They have been asked to bring their unique fragrance and beauty to the world!

When you choose to judge others for their differences, know that they are as much a part of the garden as you are. When you judge another, you judge the garden, and most importantly, you judge the Creator of the garden. Let go, and see difference as a strong thread that holds us together instead of a weak thread that keeps us apart. Harmony is the beauty of the fabric of the world, and if we honor it, we serve humanity well. If we fight it, we fight the harmony, beauty, and infinite nature of God.

CHAPTER 39

—⁓◦⌒◦⌒◦⌒◦⁓—

The Higher Vision of Peace

"World peace begins with inner peace.
Inner peace is finding Me."

For just a moment, imagine. Imagine each human being functioning from a place of peace, presence, God-centered awareness, and listening to God. What would the world look like? Would there be such hate and violence among peoples and countries?

From a place of inner peace and God-centered awareness, there is unity—no sense of false self, or ego, obtained by standing firm with divisive beliefs. Human beings honor one another's differences, seeing them as diverse and revering their beauty. The colors that each individual expresses become the infinite bright colors of blossoms in the garden of the world—harmonic components to a chord, flavors to a recipe, and infinite forms of beauty. This is harmony. This is also the dream of peace.

We all see the signs that our earth is in serious turmoil as we watch aggression, disorder, and chaos veil our hopes and prayers for peace. All countries see increased violence inflicted from one human being upon another. This is done only to increase a human being's sense of false self, or ego, in order for that person to feel superior to the other. On a collective level, the structures created by human beings who work together for a common cause can do exactly the same injustice—only in a more powerful and intimidating way. Collective false selves, or egos, sometimes work together to create the same sense of self an individual creates when he or she inflicts violence upon another.

Without the shells of our egos dividing us, we are all innately goodness. The ego shell has given us a sense of false self. Let us go deeper within to find the beauty of our sense of Self—the Self that is the essence of who we are—not what we are or what we do. The Self is innately beauty, love, pure goodness, unity, and compassion. This is the Self that we are each wishing to find. And yet, it is right underneath the layers of untruths our false selves have come to believe about who we are.

The way to create world peace is by creating inner peace. It is the nature of the world of the unmanifested to start from the heart and reach outward. Inner knowing and inner wisdom from God are uncovered within us and move outward to others through *being*.

Inner peace begins within our hearts and moves outward in the same way—outward toward one another, infinitely, moving from within to without, gently flowing through *being* to those with open hearts.

How does one open his heart when there is so much anger in the world? How does one go to a place of inner peace when there is so much to do to fill up one's life? It starts with letting go of what we do not need—all that is filling up our space—and finding the emptiness to be. It means not scheduling so many appointments in one day or activities each night. What does this do for us? It allows what is in our lives to be seen from a place of space. Why space? We see more clearly things that are not crowded together with other things. With space, our tasks are seen in their own light. This space is needed to see each thread of unique beauty and for our hearts to allow God to work through us.

It means waking up in the morning excited to see something as simple as the sun rising in the east or the beauty of snowflakes falling from the sky. It means listening to our fellow humans without judgment or expectation, listening deeply enough to hear what is unspoken beneath the words. It begins by focusing on an eternal present moment and not on an imaginary future—or a finished past—and meeting God where He stands in the present moment.

We begin by presence—staying in the now moment. We begin to release obsessive thoughts and stories, for we realize that they reinforce ego and keep us from our hearts. From the stillness of silence, we listen to the heart speaking to us. We soon find the answers it gives us are the answers for which we have been waiting. We learn to uncover deeper, innate wisdom and love—the essence of who we are—and we allow the heart to lead us. Inner peace is the background on that path. While walking the Way, we can allow that peace and goodness of heart to lead us straight to God.

This is not about religion, structure, a specific dogma, or words to follow. Each religion is only a vehicle to God, our Creator and the Source of all life. This is about finding who you are—the Self—and letting it lead you to God. For underneath all the mind stuff is heart stuff and your true Self. You must put the mind stuff, or ego, aside to get there.

I invite you on a journey of inverse thinking to uncover your Self and your essential purpose. The emptiness you feel in your life is meant to be there. It is only from that emptiness that you can uncover the sacred. It is from emptiness that God creates. It is from within this emptiness that you can hear His voice. You have been trying to fill the emptiness and space with things from the outside. Let go, and let God create a garden inside you. Spend time in the space, emptiness, and peace—and watch His garden grow! There you will find the secrets of which the ancients speak. There the answer of peace begins—not without, but within.

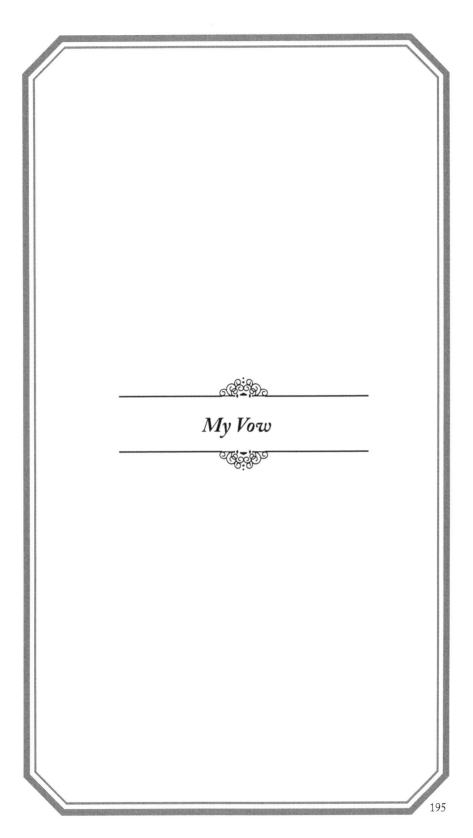

My Vow

January 18, 2009

This day, I have been with You, God.
I walked with You, and we spoke of the nothingness from which we began. We spoke of the time I was ill and I was in a cocoon, lying dead to the world, and You were laying the ground inside me for the metamorphosis that was soon to occur—
How You helped me choose to step away from the pain in my life
And how You created in me a new life—
Very slowly drawing a new creation into freedom
and oneness with You
as You and I became
We.

And we walked to the place where I tried on a new heart,
beginning to wear it through the spring in my step, the eagerness to walk on to beauty,
while we sent messages of love to the trees, watching them sway in return.
I remember the lake back then with Your story of the ripples and how You wished us to touch the entire world this very simple way.
There were days when the lake was a storm of waves and days when only two or three ripples could be seen in the calm.
This, You told me, was the barometer of our work.
And if I ever wished to know if I were doing as You wished, I was to look deep into the lake, deep into the ripples.

And You told me that You wished me to help You to bring the world to peace. You asked me to "teach them to hear Me," and we have begun to teach them, dear God.

Together, we have worked with these—Your children—my brothers and sisters who come to us.

Each of them has heard Your voice, dear God.

Each of them now has a relationship with You that is deeper and more intimate than they ever thought possible.

Please send to me whom You wish me to bring to You next, dear God.

I will always be ready.

Today as we walked, the lake was silent, frozen in thick ice with only small areas where water could be seen. The lake was quietly taking to its new form as I was taking to mine.

High on a treetop across the bridge was a large hawk sitting proudly on the branch looking down at me.

Was that You standing over me, guiding me on the Way?

We walked on and saw tall tree branches glistening in the sunshine. If the temperature had been lower, I would have thought them frozen in place. But today was a winter taste of springtime with higher temperatures,

and the glistening came from Your light alone.

It stopped my feet from walking past its awesome beauty.

I had to stand to face Your sparkling light.

As we walked to the meditation garden, a goose on our lake cried out in a lonely voice. All his friends were tending the countryside by the lake, looking for signs of spring morsels.

He stood on the ice, skating alone—a small goose on a lake of wonder.

Didn't he realize it was a field of infinite possibility?

I walked on into our garden and sat on a rock bench in the sunshine. For the first time this new year, I inhaled Your fragrant springtime call.

You were beckoning me to the place mystics go, a place with the fragrance of hope and peace. I knew it well.

I recognized Your fragrance, as it has called me before from more distant places in my mind.

We sat there together, You and I—and for that long while, we were one.

We remembered all the times of recent past when we sat together on that bench—
future unknown but open to the Infinite. And today, once again, new lands of peace called to me—
new terrain that we must walk together.

There is always comfort and the spirit of adventure in Your call as it awakens this heart to new pastures and new possibilities.

I awakened to You more deeply once again in that moment, a glorious reminder that wherever You take me, my heart finds peace.

The girl who sat with You today found her Self sitting there forever changed from our last sitting in the garden—
many of her hopes and dreams made true by Your loyalty and love. And she wondered how she will be the next day she ventures out into that garden, with Your fragrance luring her to stay.

Will Your freshness entice her further to help You change the world the way our heart so desires?

Will she be in despair because this journey eludes her?

Or will we together have accomplished what You asked of her in Your beautiful form and grace?

You told me once "We are changing our world,"
and I sat with that, making sure to re-choose this wish.

Always You remind me I am free to make a different choice.
Always You dance away from me when the meditation of a choice becomes mindful and difficult.
But always I choose You—
over and over and over again — above this world and its temptations.
I choose You—in Your elegant beauty, Your depth of love and meaning in my life, and Your present moments that live on in my heart forever.

Dear, dear God,
I will always choose You.

Your beloved daughter,
Frannie Rose

Epilogue

Years have passed since God gave me what We call my first creed—sharing with me what He wishes for me to do to help Him in my life. Through the years, the fire of God's voice has grown in my heart. At the time of this printing, I serve as co-founder and spiritual teacher of a nonprofit organization called One Simple Voice. I work with students of all religions, but I especially enjoy working with the clergy and religious whom God has generously sent to me, for in my creed, this is what He asked me to do.

Everything God told me has begun. I am teaching those who wish to hear God's voice about their journeys, their obstacles, and how to hear God. The program I share with them is one of intensive contemplative prayer through journaling, a daily process in which students learn to listen and record the beautiful and gentle messages God speaks to them. Through this practice, the students begin to feel a relationship with God. And through this relationship, they each feel a consciousness of the union with God.

We have created together a program called Sacred Conversations, in which students share God's voice and message with each other, coming together as one in God. The essential message each individual hears from God is the same. This innovative project has been shared with congregations of nuns, groups of spiritual seekers, and gatherings of priests who hear God's voice. We have found that God brings us all to the center—peace—and shares the same message with all of us.

Joyfully, I now work alongside Bishop Richard Hanifen, the bishop I met at the hospital dinner. As partners in the mission I co-founded with Sister Nancy Hoffman, we and others who have joined us work together to create a better world—one that listens to and shares *One Simple Voice*—God's voice. With so much joy and wonder, profoundly, I share with you that all of God's words have come true. I realize that most amazing of all is a far greater reality: all that has happened within this book is not my story. All along, it has been *His-story*.

About the Author

Spiritual teacher, inspirational speaker, and author Frannie Rose has always focused on the art of healing. Frannie received her graduate degree in speech and language pathology from the University of Arizona. As a speech and language pathologist, she worked with stroke and brain-injured patients in Arizona and Colorado. In this experience, she discovered the joy of helping those in need.

After her career was derailed by the sudden onset of an unknown illness at the age of thirty-two, Frannie spent seventeen years bedridden. She had to give up her career as a speech pathologist and business owner and became limited in her role as a mother to young toddlers. Faced with these losses, Frannie was forced to make the choice to surrender to a God in whom she hardly believed or to commit suicide. She chose to live.

From the trials and tribulations of these lost years, Frannie began forging a new life. She wrote her first book, *Fixing Frannie*, published in 2001 by GMA Publishing. In 2003, she authored an inspirational column, *Ask Frannie Online*, for several online organizations. As her own wellness increased, she began to focus solely on her journey with God. The events that Frannie describes in *The Invitation: Uncovering God's Longing to Be Heard* took her on a spiritual path of enlightenment and discovery which she now shares with others in her teachings, writings, and workshops.

Currently, Frannie is the co-founder and spiritual teacher of the nonprofit organization named after God's voice, One Simple Voice (OSV), located in the offices of the Catholic Diocese of Colorado Springs. Through OSV, she teaches in retreats and workshops for interfaith groups, religious groups, and other organizations, and she is invited to make presentations for other professional speaking engagements. She also carries a full-time load of spiritual students, including diocesan priests who serve more than 160,000 parishioners. Her following includes people from all walks of life, including religious clergy, bishops, nuns, those who wander, high-powered executives, those with addictions, and the unemployed. Frannie is most inspired by God to teach clergy how to hear God's voice—with the purpose of breathing God's words, acceptance, and peace into organized religion.

Frannie continues to walk through the greenery every day, devoting hours of each day to a mystical journey of peace and union with God. With her children now fully grown, she lives with her husband in the mountains of Colorado in a world she describes as "one filled with wonder and the true essence of life." Frannie's deepest wishes are echoes of God's wish: a world where there is peace and harmony as every soul listens to His voice. She wishes for each soul to know that a mystical journey such as hers is possible for anyone.

Please visit www.FrannieRose.com or www.OneSimpleVoice.org to learn more about Frannie Rose or to participate in a retreat or online event hosted by One Simple Voice.

Made in the USA
Middletown, DE
29 March 2016